W9-AAX-638

CONTEMPORARY
ISSUES
COMPANION

Gun Violence

Other Books of Related Interest:

Opposing Viewpoints Series

Domestic Violence

Gun Control

Current Controversies

School Violence

Violence Against Women

At Issue Series

Guns and Crime

Gun Violence

Stefan Kiesbye, Book Editor

GREENHAVEN PRESS
A part of Gale, Cengage Learning

Detroit • New York • San Francisco • New Haven, Conn • Waterville, Maine • London

GALE
CENGAGE Learning

Christine Nasso, *Publisher*
Elizabeth Des Chenes, *Managing Editor*

© 2008 Greenhaven Press, a part of Gale, Cengage Learning.

Gale and Greenhaven Press are registered trademarks used herein under license.

For more information, contact:
Greenhaven Press
27500 Drake Rd.
Farmington Hills, MI 48331-3535
Or you can visit our Internet site at gale.cengage.com

ALL RIGHTS RESERVED.
No part of this work covered by the copyright herein may be reproduced, transmitted, stored, or used in any form or by any means graphic, electronic, or mechanical, including but not limited to photocopying, recording, scanning, digitizing, taping, Web distribution, information networks, or information storage and retrieval systems, except as permitted under Section 107 or 108 of the 1976 United States Copyright Act, without the prior written permission of the publisher.

For product information and technology assistance, contact us at

Gale Customer Support, 1-800-877-4253
For permission to use material from this text or product, submit all requests online at www.cengage.com/permissions

Further permissions questions can be emailed to permissionrequest@cengage.com

Articles in Greenhaven Press anthologies are often edited for length to meet page requirements. In addition, original titles of these works are changed to clearly present the main thesis and to explicitly indicate the author's opinion. Every effort is made to ensure that Greenhaven Press accurately reflects the original intent of the authors. Every effort has been made to trace the owners of copyrighted material.

Cover photograph reproduced by permission of Image copyright April Turner, 2008. Used under license from Shutterstock.com.

LIBRARY OF CONGRESS CATALOGING-IN-PUBLICATION DATA

Gun violence / Stefan Kiesbye, book editor.
p. cm. -- (Contemporary issues companion)
Includes bibliographical references and index.
ISBN-13: 978-0-7377-3946-6 (hardcover)
ISBN-13: 978-0-7377-3947-3 (pbk.)
1. Gun control--United States--Juvenile literature. 2. Violent crimes--United States--Juvenile literature. 3. Firearms ownership--Government policy--United States--Juvenile literature. I. Kiesbye, Stefan.
HV7436.G8764 2008
364.150973--dc22

2008007485

Printed in the United States of America
1 2 3 4 5   12 11 10 09 08
ED173

Contents

Chapter 3: Personal Perspectives on Gun Violence

Chapter 4: Deterring Gun Violence

Foreword

In the news, on the streets, and in neighborhoods, individuals are confronted with a variety of social problems. Such problems may affect people directly: A young woman may struggle with depression, suspect a friend of having bulimia, or watch a loved one battle cancer. And even the issues that do not directly affect her private life—such as religious cults, domestic violence, or legalized gambling—still impact the larger society in which she lives. Discovering and analyzing the complexities of issues that encompass communal and societal realms as well as the world of personal experience is a valuable educational goal in the modern world.

Effectively addressing social problems requires familiarity with a constantly changing stream of data. Becoming well informed about today's controversies is an intricate process that often involves reading myriad primary and secondary sources, analyzing political debates, weighing various experts' opinions—even listening to firsthand accounts of those directly affected by the issue. For students and general observers, this can be a daunting task because of the sheer volume of information available in books, periodicals, on the evening news, and on the Internet. Researching the consequences of legalized gambling, for example, might entail sifting through congressional testimony on gambling's societal effects, examining private studies on Indian gaming, perusing numerous web sites devoted to Internet betting, and reading essays written by lottery winners as well as interviews with recovering compulsive gamblers. Obtaining valuable information can be time-consuming—since it often requires researchers to pore over numerous documents and commentaries before discovering a source relevant to their particular investigation.

Greenhaven's Contemporary Issues Companion series seeks to assist this process of research by providing readers with useful and pertinent information about today's complex issues. Each volume in this anthology series focuses on a topic of current interest, presenting informative and thought-provoking selections written from a wide variety of viewpoints. The readings selected by the editors include such diverse sources as personal accounts and case studies, pertinent factual and statistical articles, and relevant commentaries and over–views. This diversity of sources and views, found in every Contemporary Issues Companion, offers readers a broad perspective in one convenient volume.

In addition, each title in the Contemporary Issues Companion series is designed especially for young adults. The selections included in every volume are chosen for their accessibility and are expertly edited in consideration of both the reading and comprehension levels of the audience. The structure of the anthologies also enhances accessibility. An introductory essay places each issue in context and provides helpful facts such as historical background or current statistics and legislation that pertain to the topic. The chapters that follow organize the material and focus on specific aspects of the book's topic. Every essay is introduced by a brief summary of its main points and biographical information about the author. These summaries aid in comprehension and can also serve to direct readers to material of immediate interest and need. Finally, a comprehensive index allows readers to efficiently scan and locate content.

The Contemporary Issues Companion series is an ideal launching point for research on a particular topic. Each anthology in the series is composed of readings taken from an extensive gamut of resources, including periodicals, newspapers, books, government documents, the publications of private and public organizations, and Internet web sites. In these volumes, readers will find factual support suitable for use in reports, debates, speeches, and research papers. The anthologies also facilitate further research, featuring a book and periodical bibliography and a list of organizations to contact for additional information.

A perfect resource for both students and the general reader, Greenhaven's Contemporary Issues Companion series is sure to be a valued source of current, readable information on social problems that interest young adults. It is the editors' hope that readers will find the Contemporary Issues Companion series useful as a starting point to formulate their own opinions about and answers to the complex issues of the present day.

Introduction

"A well regulated Militia, being necessary to the security of a free State, the right of the people to keep and bear Arms, shall not be infringed." The meaning of the Second Amendment, penned and ratified in 1789, is, after more than two hundred years, still open for interpretation. The National Rifle Association (NRA) claims that the amendment gives individuals the right to own and carry any number of firearms. Gun control proponents state that the amendment was never meant to be so broadly applied, and merely granted states the right to maintain militias. They further contend that the amendment was a product of its time, when the United States was a rural society and had only recently gained, and defended, its independence. In their opinion, the amendment is hardly applicable to our modern and predominantly urban society, which has seen a proliferation of guns in general and handguns in particular.

The United States reports approximately ten thousand gun-related fatalities annually, a staggering number that makes gun ownership and gun control such a fiercely debated topic. Ever since the Columbine High School shooting in 1999, school and campus massacres have gained notoriety, but gun-related deaths are daily occurrences. On June 26, 2006, in East Brunswick, New Jersey, twelve-year-old Alexander Khoudiakov died from a gunshot wound to the head. He and another boy were playing at his friend's house, when, according to the Middlesex County prosecutor's office, a single round from a .38 caliber Smith & Wesson "penetrated Alexander's right eye and severed the brain stem, killing him instantly."

Alexander's friend was living with his dad and grandmother, and the weapon was kept in the bedroom the boy shared with his father. At the time of Alexander's death, the weapon was pointed directly at his face, and the shooter was charged with aggravated assault. There was no intent to kill, since the boy thought his father's weapon was unloaded, but because he could gain access to the gun so easily, his ignorance proved costly.

After the shooting, ninety-eight firearms and over sixteen hundred rounds of ammunition were found in the house. In the bedroom, police found twenty-one handguns and four rifles. Five of the weapons were loaded. Twenty-nine rifles were removed from the grandmother's bedroom. Both father and grandmother were charged by the prosecutor's office with "(1) endangering the welfare of children as second and third degree offenses; (2) the fourth degree offense of possession of a large capacity ammunition magazine, and (3) the disorderly persons offense of failure to prevent a minor from gaining access to a loaded firearm."

The prosecutor's office noted that "there is no such thing as firearms registration or licensing in New Jersey. Rather, our law requires that a person obtain a permit before acquiring a firearm. There is, however, no separate permit requirement for possessing a firearm, however acquired, inside one's residence or place of business. Nor is there any statutory limitation on the number of firearms that can be maintained lawfully in the home or business place. As long as the weapon remains within the premises, its possession is lawful."

And a private tragedy can easily become a public one. While the numbers have been decreasing, more than three thousand students were expelled for bringing a firearm to school in the 1998–99 academic year. Reports have shown that many teenagers have easy access to guns, most often at home. In 2002, according to the Children's Defense Fund and National Center for Health Statistics, over three thousand children and teens were killed in gun-related incidents in the United States. University of North Carolina at Chapel Hill research shows that "36 percent of the people reporting gun ownership and younger children in the home admitted to keeping the firearms loaded. 45 percent didn't store their guns locked, and 57 percent failed to store them in a locked compartment." In other areas, parents did much better: "99 percent had a smoke alarm, 72 percent capped electrical outlets and 72 percent kept poisonous substances out of children's reach." Yet when it came to weapons, parents seemed to turn a blind eye to the grave danger they posed to their kids.

To curb the possible risks, some states, among them Florida, have adopted Child Access Prevention (CAP) laws, which hold adults criminally liable for unsafe firearm storage in the environment of children. A study has shown that in Florida, the laws have contributed to the decrease of unintentional firearm deaths to children.

The American Academy of Pediatrics recommends "that the safest way to avoid firearm injury in the home is to remove guns from the home." If parents insist on keeping guns in the house, they should unload them and lock them up. In addition, ammunition should be stored separately and locked up as well.

Alexander Khoudiakov's death could have been prevented. Parents have to become aware that keeping firearms in the house puts their own children, and possibly the children of others, in acute danger. No matter their stance on guns, parents have to take the first step and keep their children safe. *Contemporary Issues Companion: Gun Violence* explores the extent of the problem in the United States, examines the causes of gun violence along with possible solutions, and includes the personal narratives of those affected by gun violence firsthand.

CHAPTER 1

Gun Violence in the United States

Gun Violence in the United States Is Lethal

David Hemenway

In this viewpoint, David Hemenway compares gun violence in the United States to that in several industrialized nations and finds that the difference is not in the number of gun-related incidents but in shooting fatalities, with the United States having the worst statistics by far. The author finds that the rise of fatalities is linked to an increase in the number of handguns owned and available to everyone. David Hemenway is professor of health policy at the Harvard School of Public Health and director of Harvard's Injury Control Research Center and Youth Violence Prevention Center.

Perhaps the most appropriate international comparisons are those between the United States and other developed "frontier" countries where English is spoken: Australia, Canada, and New Zealand. These four nations have roughly similar per capita incomes, cultures, and histories (including the violent displacement of indigenous populations). In 1992, the rates of property crime and violent crime were comparable across these four countries; however, by the end of the twentieth century, with the decline in U.S. crime, crime rates were actually lower in the United States than in these other countries. What distinguishes the United States is its high rate of lethal violence. In 1992 our murder rate was five times higher than the average of these three other countries; in 1999–2000 it was still about three times higher. In contrast to these other nations, most of our murderers use guns. Comparisons with other high-income countries make our gun/lethal violence problem look even worse.

David Hemenway, *Private Guns, Public Health*. Ann Arbor: University of Michigan Press, 2004. Copyright © 2004 by David Hemenway. All rights reserved. Reproduced by permission.

Canada, Australia, and New Zealand all have many guns, though not nearly as many handguns as the United States. The key difference is that these other countries do a much better job of regulating their guns. Their experience and that of all high-income nations shows that when there are reasonable restrictions on guns, gun injuries need not be such a large public health problem. Their experience also shows that it is possible to live in a society with many guns yet one in which relatively few crimes are committed with guns.

A Public Health Issue

A nation may be judged by how well it protects its children. In terms of lethal violence, the United States does very badly. For example, a comparison of violent deaths of five- to fourteen-year-olds in the United States and in the other twenty-five high-income countries during the 1990s shows that the United States has much higher suicide and homicide rates, almost entirely because of the higher gun death rates. The United States has ten times the firearm suicide rate and the same nonfirearm suicide rate as these other countries, and the United States has seventeen times the firearm homicide rate and only a somewhat higher nonfirearm homicide rate. Our unintentional firearm death rate is nine times higher.

Of particular concern was the rise in children's violent deaths in the early 1990s. For example, between 1950 and 1993, the overall death rate for U.S. children under age fifteen declined substantially because of decreases in deaths from both illness and unintentional injury. However, during the same period, childhood homicide rates tripled and suicide rates quadrupled; these increases resulted almost entirely from gun violence.

Though gunshot wounds often result in death, even nonfatal wounds can be devastating, leading to permanent disability. Traumatic brain injury and spinal cord injuries are two of the more serious firearm-related injuries. For example, nonfatal gunshot injuries are currently the second-leading cause of spinal cord injury in the United States; it is estimated that each year, more than two thousand individuals who are shot suffer spinal cord injuries. Spinal cord injuries from gunshot wounds also tend to be quite serious—gunshot wounds are more likely than non-violence-related traumatic spinal cord injuries (e.g., from falls or motor vehicle collisions) to lead to paraplegia and complete spinal cord injury.

The Psychological Toll

The psychological ravages of firearm trauma can be especially long-lasting. For example, compared to other traumatic injuries, gunshot wounds are more likely to lead to the development of post-traumatic stress disorder (PTSD) in children. Chronic PTSD following firearm injury is common: in one study, 80 percent of hospitalized gunshot-wound victims reported moderate or severe symptoms of post-traumatic stress eight months after the incident; in another study, 58 percent of firearm assault victims met the full diagnostic criteria for PTSD-3 thirty-six months after the incident. Even witnessing firearm violence can have serious psychological consequences. In one study, high school students who witnessed firearms suicides were at higher risk than other demographically similar students to develop psychopathology—specifically, anxiety disorders and PTSD.

The direct medical costs of gunshot wounds were estimated at six million dollars per day in the 1990s. The mean medical cost of a gunshot injury is about seventeen thousand dollars and would be higher except that the medical costs for deaths at the scene are low. Half of these costs are borne directly by U.S. taxpayers; gun injuries are the leading cause of uninsured hospital stays in the United States. The best estimate of the cost of gun violence in America, derived from asking people how much they would pay to reduce it, is about one hundred billion dollars per year.

Steps to Decrease Gun Violence

Fortunately, many reasonable policies can reduce this enormous and, among high-income nations, uniquely American public health problem—without banning all guns or handguns and without preventing responsible citizens from keeping firearms.

The Facts About Gun Ownership

The role of firearms in American history has been shrouded in myth and legend, none greater than the images of revolutionary militiamen with their trusty rifles defeating the world's most powerful nation and frontier cowboys—tough, brave, and independent—whose remarkable shooting made them memorable and heroic figures. Yet the key firearm in the Revolution was the inaccurate one-shot musket, and the regular army won the war. The militia had very limited success: George Washington considered it to be a "broken reed." . . .

Cowboys were mostly young, single, itinerant, irreligious, southern-born men who lived, worked, and played in male company. Many were combat veterans, and almost all carried firearms. Youthful irresponsibility, intoxication, and firearms led to so many murders and unintentional injuries at the end of the trail that laws were enacted to force cowboys to check their guns before they entered towns.

For today's gun enthusiasts, the citizen-soldier and the cowboy lawman remain two archetypes of American history. But what is not a myth is that America is currently awash with guns. It is estimated that there are more than two hundred million working firearms in private hands in the United States—as many guns as adults.

Handguns Become Ubiquitous

The total number of firearms in civilian hands has increased rapidly in the past forty years. Seventy percent of all new guns purchased in America during the twentieth century were bought after 1960. The type of gun purchased has also changed. In 1960, only 27 percent of the yearly additions to the gunstock were handguns; by 1994, that number had doubled to 54 percent.

While the number of guns has increased, the percentage of American households reporting that they own guns has declined markedly in recent years, from about 48 percent in 1973 to closer to 35 percent today. This decline appears in part to result from the decreasing number of adults in each household and, since 1997, from a decline in the proportion of adults who personally own firearms. However, current gun owners have been buying additional firearms; the average number of firearms owned by gun owners has been increasing in recent decades.

Facts About Gun Owners

Currently, one in four adults owns a gun of some kind, but owners of four or more guns (about 10 percent of the adult population) are in possession of 77 percent of the total U.S. stock of firearms. Many people, especially women, who live in households with a gun do not own any guns. Approximately 40 percent of adult males and 10 percent of adult females are gun owners. Even though we live in a land of firearms, the majority of males do not own guns, and only about one woman out of ten is a gun owner.

The percentage of households with long guns (rifles and shotguns) fell from 40 percent in 1973 to 32 percent in 1994, but household handgun ownership rose from 20 to 25 percent. Since the mid-1990s, even household handgun ownership has been declining. Perhaps 16 percent of U.S. adults currently own handguns.

People report owning guns primarily for hunting, target shooting, and personal protection. The reasons for ownership differ for long guns and handguns. Handguns are owned primarily for protection, while long guns are used mainly for hunting and target shooting. While all guns pose risks for injury, compared to their prevalence in the gun stock, handguns are used disproportionately in crimes, homicides, suicides, and gun accidents. Thus, some proposed gun policies focus on handguns rather than long guns.

Gun ownership varies across geographic regions; it is highest among households in the South and in the Rocky Mountain region and lowest in the Northeast. It is higher in rural areas than urban areas; it is higher among conservatives than among moderates or liberals.

Gun Owners Display Risky Behaviors

One of the most important predictors of gun ownership is whether one's parents had a gun in the home. Gun ownership is highest among those over forty years old and is more prevalent among those with higher incomes. While gun owners come from the entire spectrum of American society, people who admit to having been arrested for a nontraffic offense are more likely to own guns (37 percent versus 24 percent for those without an arrest); owners of semiautomatics are more likely than other gun owners to report that they binge drink; and combat veterans with PTSD appear more likely than other veterans to own firearms (and to engage in such potentially harmful behavior as aiming guns at family members, patrolling their property with loaded guns, and killing animals in fits of rage).

A few fringe groups of gun owners may someday pose political problems for the United States. The militia movement made the front pages after the Oklahoma City bombing in April 1995 killed 170 innocent people. Armed paramilitary organizations, formed as a result of antigovernment sentiment, interpret the U.S. Constitution for themselves. In effect, they claim liberty as their exclusive right, which sometimes includes the right to attack violently the objects of their hate. The existence of independent armed militias, sometimes filled with white supremacist rhetoric, could threaten the peaceful conduct of government and public business. These militia often identify the government itself as the enemy. By contrast, the mission of state-sponsored militia of the colonial period was in part to subdue armed insurrections against the state.

American Violence Is Lethal

It is often claimed that the United States has a crime problem. We do, but our crime rates, as determined by victimization surveys, resemble those of other high-income countries. It is often claimed that the United States has a violence problem. We do, but our violence rates resemble those of other high-income countries. What is out of line is our lethal violence, and most of our lethal violence is gun violence.

Over the past forty years, the increase in urbanization and the decline in hunting, combined with the fact that fewer adults live in each household, have resulted in a decreasing percentage of households with firearms. At the individual level, about 25 percent of adults currently own guns. On average, these individuals own more firearms than in the past, and the guns are increasingly likely to be handguns. Compared to other high-income nations, Americans own more guns, particularly handguns. And ... these guns are readily available to virtually anyone who wants one.

Gun Accidents and Homicides Are Declining

Gary Kleck and Don B. Kates

In the following viewpoint, the authors argue that contrary to common belief, accidental gun fatalities have been declining. They contend that guns inside homes do not inevitably lead to gun violence. Gary Kleck is a professor at the School of Criminology and Criminal Justice of Florida State University. Don B. Kates is a partner at the national law firm of Benenson & Kates.

Consider these facts: more than 400 percent more children under age fifteen die in drownings than in gun accidents; and twenty times as many children under age five drown in bathtubs and home swimming pools as are killed in handgun accidents. Few people *need* a bathtub (as opposed to a shower stall) or a swimming pool. If the tragedy of accidental childhood gun fatalities justifies confiscating 80 million or more handguns, or all 230 million or more firearms, do the much greater numbers of tragic childhood drownings justify a licensing system under which only the disabled and others who show they "truly need" a bathtub or swimming pool will be allowed to have them?

Note: We do not pose these as rhetorical questions having only one clear "right" answer. Reasonable people may well differ vehemently over how they ought to be answered. That is precisely why *scholars* discussing the role of firearms and other potentially harmful media in society ought to disclose the facts and raise the questions. Regrettably, the possibility that honestly informing people might lead to differing conclusions is also the reason such facts and questions are never raised by

Gary Kleck and Don B. Kates, *Armed: New Perspectives on Gun Control*. Amherst, NY: Prometheus Books, 2001. Copyright © 2001 by Gary Kleck and Don B. Kates. All rights reserved. Reprinted with permission of the publisher.

health sages who capitalize on the issue of accidental child-hood deaths to argue for banning handguns or all guns. . . .

Increased Guns, Decreased Homicides

Post–World War II American homicide rates peaked in 1979 and actually decreased over the fifteen years from 1980 to 1994. In this period the number of handguns in civilian hands increased from 51.7 million to 84.7 million, or by about 64 percent, while gun ownership overall increased about 40.5 percent, from 167.7 million to 235.6 million weapons. In this time period there was no increase at all (much less a corre-sponding increase) in homicide rates. In fact, the rate declined from 10.2 per 100,000 population in 1980 to 9.0 per 100,000 in 1994.

This was no anomaly. If one pushes out the study period to twenty-five years (i.e., the period from 1973 to 1997), the lack of correlation between homicide rates and firearms avail-ability appears even more stark. Over that period homicides decreased by 27.7 percent (from 9.4 to 6.8 in 100,000 of population), despite an approximate 160 percent increase in the number of handguns owned by civilians (from 36.9 mil-lion to 94.9), and a 103 percent increase in civilian gun own-ership (from 128 million to 254.5 million weapons) overall. The consistent, characteristic pattern of the entire postwar pe-riod has been that murder rates and firearms acquisition pat-terns have been uncorrelated, with only the relatively brief pe-riod from the mid-1960s to the late 1970s as the exception.

The increases in firearms over this period, moreover, have far outstripped population increases. In 1973 there were 610.3 guns (175.9 handguns) per 1,000 population; by 1994 the fig-ures were 905 guns and 325.2 handguns per 1,000 population, respectively.

Of course within the 1973 to 1997 period homicide rates fluctuated considerably, rising in some years, falling in others. In themselves, these fluctuations provide further evidence that homicide rates are independent of gun availability levels. Gun, particularly handgun, availability levels exhibit no comparable fluctuation. While homicide rates rose and fell, handgun ownership only rose. Each year from 1973 through 1997 the existing stock increased by between 1.7 and 3.7 million new handguns. These increases were accompanied by a long-term decline in murder.... Once again, these are facts that readers whose information comes from health advocacy literature will never learn.

Likewise never discussed (at least in connection with breakdowns of rates of firearms ownership by race) in the health advocacy literature is that the white homicide rate has steadily fallen since 1980. The apparent increase in American homicide from the mid-1980s on is due entirely to that steady fall in white homicide being offset by a vast increase in homicide in drug and crime-ridden, poverty-stricken inner cities. Inner-city and minority youth homicide is a regular theme in the antigun health literature. Of course, health sages never note that the whites whose murder rate is declining are far more likely to own guns per capita than African Americans in general, and that black gun ownership is *lowest* in the inner cities....

The Actual Causes of Murder

In sum, increased firearm availability to honest, responsible people (of any race) does not cause increased violence; neither is lower availability to such people *associated* with lower violence. Taken together or separately, data on firearm availability for the nation as a whole, and for discrete geographic or demographic subpopulations, discredit the shibboleth [a commonplace idea] that "the possession of guns" is "the primary cause" of murder. The actual cause is hopelessness, poverty, and a lack of substantial employment opportunities—other than competing in the murderous drug trade. Studies suggest black rates of homicide and other violence are no greater than those of similarly situated whites. . . .

Murderers-as-Gun-Owners Myth

It simply isn't true that previously law-abiding citizens commit most murders or many murders or virtually any murders; and so disarming them could not eliminate most or many or virtually any murders. Homicide studies show that murderers are not ordinary citizens, but extreme aberrants of whom it is unrealistic to assume they will have any more compunction about flouting gun laws than about murder.

Young People Are Victims and Perpetrators of Gun Violence

Alfred Blumstein

Young people make up most of the victims and perpetrators of violent crimes. In this viewpoint, Alfred Blumstein looks for possible answers and finds that the myth of the young "superpredator" doesn't correspond with reality. Instead he finds evidence that other factors, such as the proliferation of handguns, the rise of the illegal drug market, and an increase in gun carrying among youth, contribute to the dire statistics. Alfred Blumstein is a professor of Urban Systems and Operations Research at Carnegie Mellon University.

The period from 1985 to 2000 saw some sharp swings in the rate of violence in the United States. Much of that swing is attributable to changes in violence committed by young people, primarily against other young people. Beginning in 1985, the rates of homicide and robbery committed by people under age 20 began to rise dramatically, as did the use of handguns to commit those crimes. This increase in violence peaked in the early 1990s, then fell significantly by the end of the 1990s.

Although youth violence has declined in recent years, a rash of school shootings in the late 1990s generated significant public concern and attention from policy-makers. This concern is not new—rhetoric about violent youth has captured public attention over the last two decades. Accordingly, federal and state legislators have sought to impose stiffer penalties on youth who are found guilty of violent crimes, by mandating, for instance, that juveniles who commit violent crimes be

Alfred Blumstein, "Youth, Guns, and Violent Crime," *The Future of Children*, vol. 12, August 19, 2007, pp. 40–51. Copyright 2007 Brookings Institution. Reproduced by permission.

tried in adult court rather than juvenile court. In particular, in 2000 California voters passed, by a two to one majority, Proposition 21, which increases the range of offenses for which juvenile offenders as young as age 14 will be tried and sentenced as adults.

This punitive response to youth violence follows from public rhetoric that labeled a whole generation of youth as "superpredators." This labeling occurred during the peak of the youth violence epidemic, partly in response to outrageous killings by very young people. The superpredator label suggested that the new generation of young people were out of control, beyond redemption, and had little regard for human life or victims' pain and suffering. Some commentators argued that particularly aggressive steps were needed to keep them under control.

Whether this is an appropriate response to youth violence depends upon the answers to two key questions. First, to what degree was the increase in violence of the late 1980s and early 1990s attributable to youth? Second, to what degree was that growth attributable to a new group of superpredator youth who were inherently more violent than previous generations of young people? . . .

Young People and the Violence Epidemic

Despite public perceptions about increased crime and violence in the United States, a detailed examination of homicide and robbery rates from 1965 through 2000 shows that these rates have not changed dramatically over time. What has changed is the number of homicides committed by young people. Indeed, the increase in homicide rates in the late 1980s and early 1990s was driven entirely by a rise in youth homicide with handguns.

Homicide Rates in the General Population

The homicide rate in the United States oscillated between 8 and 10 per 100,000 population from 1970 to 1995. In 1980, it peaked at 10.2 murders per 100,000 population, and by 1985 it had fallen to 7.9. It then climbed a full 24% to reach a peak of 9.8 in 1991, and has been declining markedly since then, reaching 5.5 in 2000. The last change represents a drop of 44% since 1991, to a level that is lower than any annual rate since 1965. The robbery rate has followed a very similar pattern, reaching its peaks and troughs within one year of those of the murder trends. The robbery rate has also displayed a steady decline since its 1991 peak, and the 2000 rate is lower than any since 1968.

Despite the fairly sharp swings it is striking how flat the trend lines for homicide and robbery were before the declines of the 1990s. Homicide and robbery rates jumped up and down from year to year, but they did not change dramatically between 1970 and 1993. The stability of these rates stands in marked contrast to the general view of the American public—and the rhetoric of many political candidates, who suggested throughout the 1990s that crime rates were getting out of hand and that crime was becoming an increasingly serious threat. Indeed, even the steady decline in violent crime rates since 1993 has not fully eased these concerns. . . .

Youth's Contribution to Homicide Rate

When the homicide rate is disaggregated by age, it becomes clear that the increase in homicide after 1985 was driven almost entirely by a significant increase in homicides committed by juveniles (those under age 18) and youth (those between the ages of 18 and 24). . . .

For all ages below 20, the 1993 homicide arrest rate was more than double the 1985 rate. For example, the murder arrest rate for 15-year-olds in 1993 was triple what the rate had been in 1985.

In contrast, adults have displayed a continuing decline in homicide arrest rates since the mid-1970s. By 1993, when homicide arrests among young people reached their peak levels, arrest rates among the over-30 population had declined by about 20% from the 1985 level. The decline continued into the 1990s, and by 2000 it had reached a level about 50% below the 1985 rate.

Thus, the 1991 peak in aggregate homicide rates came about solely because of increased violence by youth under age 25; homicide rates for youth were increasing much faster than the rates for adults over age 25 were declining. Because homicide rates for young and old offenders alike decreased after 1993, the aggregate rate continued to fall—and fall rapidly. The decrease since 1993 is due to both the recent sharp drop in violent crime among young people, and to the continuing decline in violent crime among older persons.

Racial Differences in the Homicide Rate

In addition to age differences, there were important racial differences in the growth of homicides—particularly an increase in homicides among young African Americans, both as offenders and as victims. . . . Among African Americans, handgun use grew much more sharply than for youth generally; the number of handgun homicides among African Americans in this age group [ages eighteen to twenty-four] nearly tripled from 1984 to 1993. Although some growth also occurred in handgun homicides by white and Hispanic youth, that increase was far less dramatic. Among all youth, there was no comparable growth in the use of other weapons to commit homicides. . . .

Contributing Factors to the Epidemic

Though the superpredator theory has attracted widespread public attention, other factors—most notably the availability of handguns, increased weapon carrying among young people, and the explosive growth of illegal drug markets—more likely fueled the increase in youth homicide. This section reviews each of these factors in detail.

The Role of Handguns

Since 1985, the weapons involved in settling disputes among young people have changed dramatically, from fists or knives to handguns. Youth use of handguns to commit suicides and robberies also has risen significantly. More recently, young people have begun to use semiautomatic pistols with much greater firepower and lethality.

The growing use of lethal handguns is reflected in changes in the weapons involved in homicides by young people in different race and age groups. Beginning in 1985, there was a sharp growth in the firearm homicide rate among young people. That rise in firearm homicides changed what had been a flat trend in homicides committed by youth to a sharply rising one—with the rise sharpest for youth ages 18 and under. There was no comparable growth in homicides committed with other weapons. This suggests that the use of handguns, rather than an increase in violent attitudes among young people, is largely responsible for the increase in violent crime in the late 1980s and early 1990s.

A review of the weapons used in homicides committed by young people, especially those under age 18, clearly shows this sharp rise in the use of firearms to commit homicides. . . .

Not only did young people under age 25 account for all of the growth in homicides in the post-1985 period, but that growth stemmed entirely from the increase in homicides committed with handguns. Furthermore, most of the growth was accounted for by youth under age 20. Clearly, the sharp rise in the use of handguns in youth and juvenile homicide is crucial in explaining the increase in the aggregate homicide rate in the late 1980s and early 1990s. Comparably, the more recent sharp decrease in handgun homicides by young people is an important factor in the overall decline since the early 1990s.

Guns Increase Violent Crime

Firearms have also played an important role in the growth in robberies. No incident-based data source is available for robberies as it is for homicides, but the aggregate statistics indicate a clear rise in the fraction of robberies committed with firearms from 1989 to 1991. During that time—precisely the period when there was a major increase in young people's involvement in robbery—the total rate of firearm robberies increased by 42%. Over the same period, the rate of nonfirearm robberies increased by only 5%.

These observations suggest that the growth in homicides by young people was attributable much more to the weapons that found their way into their hands than to the emergence of inadequately socialized cohorts of superpredators, as some have claimed. If the cohorts were indeed more vicious, then one would expect to see an increase in homicide with all forms of weapons, rather than just handguns. The findings strongly suggest that teenagers committed crimes and fought as they always had, but that the greater lethality of handguns led to a greater number of disputes resulting in homicides. It was the availability of handguns, rather than a new generation of superpredators, that contributed to the growth in youth violence.

Trends in Weapons Carrying

Throughout the late 1980s and early 1990s, an increasing number of young people carried handguns, likely helping to fuel a rise in youth homicide rates. Even though federal law prohibits the sale of handguns to people under age 21 or possession of handguns by juveniles, it is surprisingly common for young people to carry guns. For example, an estimated 10% of male high school students have carried a gun in the previous 30 days. Gun carrying is even more common in high-crime areas, where 25% of male teenagers carry guns, and among high-risk groups. More than 80% of male juvenile offenders report having possessed a gun.

Young people who carry guns report that their major reason for doing so is concern for their own safety. In one national survey, 43% of high school students who reported carrying a gun within the past 12 months claimed they carried it primarily for protection. However, when disputes arise, no matter how minor, youth who carry guns may use them preemptively, especially if they suspect that their adversaries also have guns.

The Role of Drug Markets

The rise of illegal drug markets—most notably markets for crack cocaine—also was a likely factor behind the increase in youth gun homicide, especially among African American young people in the inner city. When youth involved in illegal drug markets began carrying guns for protection and dispute resolution, other young people within the community began carrying guns as well. This diffusion of guns from the drug markets into the larger community led to an increase in gun carrying, resulting in more gun homicides.

A serious drug problem, fueled by the introduction of crack cocaine into urban areas, began to emerge in the United States in the early 1980s, and then accelerated significantly in the mid- to late 1980s. The arrest rate of nonwhite (primarily African American) adults for drug offenses started to rise in the early 1980s, then grew appreciably after 1985 with the wide distribution of crack cocaine, especially in urban ghettos. . . .

One explanation for this rather dramatic increase in weapons arrest rates and youth violence assigns a central role to illegal drug markets, which appear to operate in a reasonable equilibrium with the demand for drugs, despite massive efforts over the past 15 years to attack the supply side. The drug industry recruited juveniles because they were willing to work more cheaply than adults, they were less vulnerable to the punishments imposed by the adult criminal justice system, and they were often willing to take risks that more mature adults would eschew.

In addition, there was a rapid growth of incarceration of older drug sellers—especially the African Americans who constituted the dominant group of sellers in the crack markets. Between 1980 and 1996, the incarceration rate in state prisons for drug offenses grew by a factor of 10. This growth in incarceration for drug crimes created a strong demand for new recruits as replacements. Moreover, the rapid growth in demand for crack transactions—spurred by new users for whom powder cocaine had been inaccessible because of its high cost, and by an increase in transactions per consumer—made the illegal drug markets anxious for a new labor supply. Finally, the economic plight of many urban black juveniles, who saw no other satisfactory route to economic sustenance made them particularly vulnerable to the lure of employment in the crack markets. . . .

The Government Has to Act

The United States has seen the consequences of easy youth access to guns in the rise of handgun homicides by young people starting in about 1985 and continuing until a peak in 1993. The entire growth in homicides over that period was attributable to young people with handguns. The subsequent decline in overall homicide rates has been dominated by the decline in handgun homicides by young people, and homicide rates among juveniles and youth are now just about back to where they were in 1985.

A number of complex factors have contributed to the recent decline in young people's violence: the shrinking of illegal drug markets, a robust economy that provided youth with legitimate employment and an incentive to conform to the law, and varied efforts to control youth access to guns.

However, having guns available to young people who lack skill in handling them and are insensitive to their lethal potential can be terrifying. The question remains: What can be done to sustain the recent declines in violent crimes committed by youth?

One answer is clear. As this article illustrates, youth homicide rates are sensitive to enforcement of gun control laws, as well as larger economic factors. Although economic downturns (and perhaps the emergence of new drug markets) are inevitable, government has at least some power to regulate the supply and use of guns by youth and other inappropriate people. Unless the government exercises that power by adopting more effective approaches to controlling youth access to guns, the United States risks seeing more lethal violence by youth the next time there is a major downturn in the economy accompanied by rapid growth of a new violence-prone drug market.

Data About Guns and Crime Are Being Suppressed

Elizabeth S. Haile

In this viewpoint, the author makes the case that data about gun violence and gun records are suppressed, withheld, or misinterpreted by gun lobbyists and a Congress fearful of losing votes from gun owners. Elizabeth S. Haile is a staff attorney for the Brady Center to Prevent Gun Violence. The center, and its legislative and grassroots affiliate, the Brady Campaign, is the nation's largest nonpartisan grassroots organization leading the fight to prevent gun violence.

It is hard to believe that in today's world, where technologically stunning crime scene investigations are featured in some of the most popular shows on television, that federal, state, and local law enforcement agencies have to operate without basic information that would allow them to quickly determine the origin of crime guns. Yet, thanks to a powerful gun lobby obsessed with secrecy, vital records held by the gun industry are either shielded from law enforcement's eyes or destroyed altogether.

The Bureau of Alcohol, Tobacco, Firearms, and Explosives (ATF), the federal agency charged with regulating the industry, has been hampered from taking effective enforcement actions against corrupt gun sellers by a series of laws enacted at the urging of the National Rifle Association (NRA)—a lobby long obsessed with secrecy. Consequently, ATF is forced to rely mainly upon voluntary compliance with federal law by members of the gun industry, and operations of the industry are shielded from public view.

Elizabeth S. Haile, *Without a Trace: How the Gun Lobby and the Government Suppress the Truth about Guns and Crime.* Washington, DC: Brady Center to Prevent Gun Violence, 2006. Copyright © 2006 by Brady Center to Prevent Gun Violence. Reproduced by permission.

The NRA has worked tirelessly to either block or weaken laws that would strengthen law enforcement's capability to regulate corrupt gun sellers and fight gun crime. The gun lobby has opposed federal laws designed to prevent the sale of guns to criminals, including: the Gun Control Act of 1968, which made it illegal to sell guns to minors and felons, established a licensing system for gun dealers, and banned the interstate sale of firearms to unlicensed persons; the 1993 Brady Law, which put in place criminal background checks for gun purchases at licensed dealers, first for handguns, then for all guns; and the 1994 Assault Weapons Act which, until its expiration in 2004, banned the sale and possession of military-style semiautomatic assault weapons.

One piece of legislation the gun lobby did support was the Firearm Owners Protection Act (FOPA), a roll-back of portions of the Gun Control Act. The FOPA limited ATF's ability to investigate corrupt gun dealers and revoke dealer licenses and exempted federally licensed dealers from certain record-keeping requirements.

The Gun Lobby's Paranoia

The gun lobby repeatedly claims that any sort of regulation of gun ownership will eventually lead to the complete confiscation of all firearms. "Registration leads to confiscation," is the NRA's mantra. Under the NRA's theory, if any governmental records are kept on firearm sales, it would inevitably lead to registration of firearms, which would lead to the confiscation of all firearms by "jack-booted government thugs" raiding people's homes.

Typical NRA advertisements hammer home the fanciful link between keeping track of firearm sales in order to prevent and solve gun crimes and the creation of a "total police state:"

"We all know their Master Plan. First, outlaw all handguns. Then register all rifles and shotguns. Finally, confiscate and destroy all rifles and shotguns. Make no mistake, these anti-gun and anti-hunting forces are working feverishly for the day when they can gather up your rifles, handguns, and shotguns and ship them off to gun-melting furnaces."

"Gun prohibition is the inevitable harbinger of oppression."

Of course there is no truth to the NRA's shrill claims, as no federal gun law has ever prevented law abiding citizens from buying a legal firearm, and state registration laws have not led to confiscation. Yet, the gun lobby's paranoia about anything related to government firearm records has led to a system of federal laws riddled with nonsensical prohibitions on state and federal law enforcement's ability to track firearm-related crime and investigate corrupt gun sellers.

Keeping Records from the Government

Federal law requires individuals who are "in the business" of selling firearms to obtain a license from ATF and keep records of all firearm purchases and sales. These transactions are required to be recorded in what is known as an "A&D" book (for Acquisition and Disposition) or computer system. A customer purchasing a firearm must also fill out and sign a Firearms Transaction Record, ATF Form 4473. This form records the buyer's name and address and type of identification shown to the gun dealer. It also requires gun buyers to answer a series of questions to determine whether the purchaser is prohibited by law from buying the gun. The information in Form 4473 is of obvious value to law enforcement if the gun in question is ever connected to criminal activity. However, these records simply sit in the dealers' shops, unless, of course, the dealer loses or misplaces them. Records containing information about particular gun sales are transmitted to the government only in limited circumstances, such as after a dealer goes out of business, or if a dealer sells more than one handgun to the same purchaser within five business days.

At the urging of the NRA, in 1979 Congress put in place restrictions in an appropriations bill prohibiting ATF from obtaining sales records from gun dealers and centralizing them. These restrictions have persisted in every appropriations bill thereafter. And in the FOPA, Congress explicitly prevented ATF from establishing any database of firearms sales. Consequently, the federal government does not have any record of the thousands of gun sales taking place at retail dealers every day. While the IRS [Internal Revenue Service] maintains records on all business and individual incomes the federal government is barred from maintaining records on the purchase and whereabouts of millions of firearms.

Moreover, the ATF is constrained from organizing even those records that ATF is allowed to obtain from dealers. Federal law requires a dealer who goes out of business to send all sales records required to be kept by law to the ATF within 30 days. However, the NRA succeeded in having Congress attach another rider to ATF appropriations legislation that prevents ATF from organizing the records in an easily accessible manner. ATF is prevented from searching the data by the purchaser's name, making it useless for law enforcement trying to research the gun purchase histories of suspects or convicted felons, or suspects who may pose a danger to the community.

These nonsensical restrictions prevent ATF from maintaining the records it needs to quickly and effectively investigate corrupt dealers or track down law enforcement leads. Because records of gun sales remain with the tens of thousands of licensed dealers and not in a centralized federal database, every time local law enforcement needs information about the origin of a gun recovered in crime, ATF must painstakingly track the gun's path through the records of the manufacturer, distributor, and (often multiple) retailers. Irresponsible sellers also frequently lose gun sales records, making complete traces of those guns impossible. The cumbersome process slows law enforcement investigations and endangers public safety.

The Short Life of Gun Records

Since passage of the Brady Law in 1993, licensed dealers must conduct criminal history background checks utilizing the Federal Bureau of Investigation's National Instant Check System (NICS), to ensure that prospective gun buyers are not prohibited purchasers. If the background check determines that the purchaser is not prohibited, a record of the check, consisting solely of an identifier number assigned to the inquiry, is kept by the Department of Justice (DOJ). But the gun lobby's obsession with secrecy is even reflected in the legislative compromises which are part of the Brady Law—the statute requires all other information on the approved purchaser and the gun purchase to be destroyed, although it does not specify that the record destruction occur immediately after the sale is approved. The record destruction requirement does not apply if the background check reveals that the purchaser is prohibited by law from buying a firearm.

Following implementation of NICS in 1998, DOJ kept the background check records on approved purchasers for six months to ensure that NICS was working properly and that felons and other prohibited purchasers were not mistakenly being approved. In July 2000, the legality of the six-month policy was affirmed by a federal court of appeals against a legal challenge brought by the National Rifle Association. In January 2001, DOJ issued a final rule shortening the record retention period to 90 days to take effect on March 1, 2001. After various postponements, the 90-day rule finally went into effect on July 3, 2001.

Three days later, DOJ, under new Attorney General John Ashcroft (a recipient of strong NRA support in his Senate campaigns), issued a new proposed rule to shorten the period further from 90 days to 24 hours, citing the need to protect "the privacy interests of law-abiding citizens." While the proposed rule was still pending, the gun lobby's allies in Congress attached a rider to an ATF appropriations bill that requires destruction of the records within 24 hours. DOJ then issued a final rule implementing the 24-hour retention period effective July 20, 2004.

In a 2002 study, the General Accounting Office [GAO] noted the dangers of requiring that NICS records be destroyed within 24 hours, concluding that such quick destruction would endanger public safety. GAO found that within one six-month period, "the FBI used retained records to initiate 235 firearm-retrieval actions, of which 228 (97 percent) could not have been initiated under the proposed next-day destruction policy." Yet, DOJ argued that the "privacy interests of law-abiding firearms purchasers" required that NICS records be destroyed. The gun lobby's allies in Congress agreed, acting to put the priorities of the secrecy-loving NRA above the needs of law enforcement.

Gun Trafficking Is a Problem

Secrecy also triumphed over law enforcement on the issue of multiple handgun sales records. It has long been recognized that multiple sales of handguns—defined in federal law as the sale of two or more handguns to the same buyer within a five business-day period—is a strong indicator that the purchaser intends to traffic the guns to the illegal market. For this reason, federal law requires federally-licensed dealers to notify ATF of every multiple handgun sale they make. Multiple sale reports are often starting points for investigations of gun trafficking.

Until the Brady Law was enacted, gun dealers were required to send multiple-sale reports only to ATF. The Brady Law imposed a new requirement that the dealer also send a copy of the report to state or local law enforcement authorities. In theory, this should allow state and local law enforcement to assist ATF or commence its own investigation. Incredibly though, the Brady Law also required the police to destroy the form and its contents within 20 days, a provision pushed by the gun lobby. In short, although the state or local police may get notice of suspicious gun sales, they have only 20 days to act before they must destroy any information relating to it. Once again, the gun lobby's friends in Congress ensured that secrecy would trump the need for valuable information that the police could use to stop the flow of guns to criminals.

Gun Laws Do Not Inhibit Gun Violence

Jordan Carleo-Evangelist

In the following viewpoint, Jordan Carleo-Evangelist highlights statistics showing that despite vast differences in gun control laws, many states have similar records on gun violence. While a ban on firearms is highly unlikely, the evidence that such a ban would reduce gun violence seems inconclusive. Jordan Carleo-Evangelist is a staff writer for the Times Union *in Albany, New York.*

Jack Buttman can sell a 9 mm Glock pistol in less time than it takes to order breakfast in a diner. It's even faster, he says, if the buyer is familiar with the one-page form for the federal background check and doesn't stop to read the questions.

Buttman, owner of Butt's Gun Sales in Billings, Mont., says he can send a buyer out the door in 12 to 20 minutes.

At any gun shop in the Capital Region [of New York state], the same sale can take as long as six months. New York is one of 12 states that require some form of permit to buy a handgun, and even permit holders wait a week to 10 days to add another gun.

Earlier this year [2004], New York state's strict gun control laws earned a solid B+ from The Brady Campaign to Prevent Gun Violence. The same report by the nation's best-known gun control advocacy group, billed as a tool to educate Americans "about how their state's leaders are doing on laws and policies that promote a reduction in gun violence," gave Montana an F.

But does it mean citizens of the Big Sky State are more at risk of gun violence?

Jordan Carleo-Evangelist, "Guns and Crime: The Great Debate," TimesUnion.com, October 17, 2004. Copyright 2007, Capital Newspapers Division of The Hearst Company, Albany, N.Y. Used by permission of Albany, N.Y. Times Union.

According to a University at Albany [State University of New York at Albany] publication of 2001 FBI statistics, the most recent available, the percentage of violent crimes committed with guns in New York state was virtually the same as in Montana—17.7 percent in New York and 17.4 percent in Montana.

Gun Laws Seem Questionable

The same is true for other states: Colorado and Connecticut, for example, have gun laws as different as New York's from Montana's, but they have about the same percentage of violent crime committed with guns.

Statistics show no clear relationship between strict gun laws and the rate of gun crimes—a fact that raises questions about the politically charged debate over gun control as a means of combating crime.

Buttman says he knows why states with diametrically opposite gun control laws have such similar crime statistics.

"There are no evil guns," Buttman said, sounding a bit exasperated over the telephone. "There are only evil people. And when you can figure out how to stop all the evil people, sir, you'll be the next Messiah."

The Sept. 13 [2004] expiration of the decade-old federal assault weapons ban once again focused attention on one of the nation's most polarized debates.

Each year about 30,000 Americans die from gunshot wounds, and another 40,000 to 50,000 are wounded. Most of the deaths result from suicides and accidents, but about a third are homicides, according to the federal Centers for Disease Control and Prevention [CDC].

All told, gunshot wounds and deaths cost more than $100 billion a year in medical treatment, lost income and other costs, according to the Center for Gun Policy and Research at Johns Hopkins University.

For decades, some states have tried to fight gun violence by a variety of laws restricting gun buying and ownership. Yet homicides involving firearms remain the nation's second leading cause of violent death, trailing only suicides involving guns.

That experience has led to a growing body of research that suggests the relationship between gun-control laws and gun crime is at best unclear. The most promising solutions to gun violence, say some researchers, may have little to do with passing new gun laws.

It's no academic debate to Patricia Gioia of Schenectady, whose 22-year-old daughter, Mary Regina, was murdered 19 years ago in California by a drifter with a history of violent crime and a rifle he shouldn't have had. She said that just because gun control laws have flaws, it doesn't mean they don't work at all. Fewer guns on the streets, she said, will save lives.

"Who's to know if (the laws) are not doing something?" said Gioia, a member of the Capital District Chapter of Parents of Murdered Children and of New Yorkers Against Gun Violence. "It's not a perfect system—it never will be. But we have to keep striving."

Though her daughter was killed with a rifle, Gioia said she understands why some people might want them for hunting. When it comes to easily concealed weapons, though, she asks, "Why does a person need a handgun?"

Can Stricter Laws Save Lives?

Vilmos Levay, a retired electro-mechanical designer for General Electric, said he needs his three registered pistols to exercise his constitutional rights and his "universal right" to defend himself. Laws that make it harder for law-abiding people to get guns abridge those rights, said Levay, 54, who . . . carries at least one handgun wherever he goes.

"What do you care what I need it for as long as I don't use it against you?" he said. "If one life is placed in jeopardy" by laws that keep regular people from getting guns, then "the law is unjust."

As the two sides continue their struggle over the place of firearms in America, a growing number of academics, politicians and policy analysts are coming to what seems to some a radical conclusion: Gun control may have at best an ambiguous impact on crime, and successful strategies for reducing gun violence must be based on new approaches that have more to do with focusing law enforcement on those who commit crimes than in restricting gun ownership.

In the end, said Jeffrey Chamberlain, former counsel to the New York State Police and co-author of a book on New York gun laws, policy-makers need to ask themselves exactly what they're trying to achieve with gun control, and how the law will achieve it.

"'What's the objective?' is always a good question to ask," said Chamberlain, who is now in private practice in Albany. "Is the objective to ban guns, or is the objective to make the streets safer? Those may be the same thing, but not necessarily."

Chamberlain quickly dismisses as impractical any suggestion that a total ban would reduce gun crime.

A Ban of Firearms Seems Unlikely

"Obviously, if we could confiscate every gun in the country we would make an impact on gun crimes. But that's trivial," he said. Political support for a ban is lacking in a nation where people own 65 million handguns and buy as many as 5 million firearms of all kinds each year, he noted, and the Second Amendment's wording makes a ban unlikely to pass constitutional muster.

Seizing firearms already in circulation, he said, is so unlikely to happen that it is "not a high-level argument." It only wastes time that could be used to find more productive solutions to violent crime, he said.

For almost 100 years, New York has licensed handgun owners as a way to limit the number of guns in circulation and to reduce crimes committed with firearms.

David Hemenway, director of Harvard University's Injury Control Research Center, has researched how availability of guns affects all types of violence, including suicides and accidents.

"The fundamental law of economics is if you raise the price of something, if you make things harder to get, fewer people get them. It doesn't mean nobody gets them," said Hemenway, author of the book *Private Guns, Public Health.*

Assessments of how well gun control achieves the goal of crime reduction vary widely. And in a debate awash with advocacy passing for science, those who study gun control caution against putting too much weight on any one statistic because so many factors influence crime.

Comparing crime statistics for any given year and laws in New York and Montana, for example, shows only that the relationship between gun control and gun crime is not as clear as many people believe.

In 2000, an independent task force created by the federal Centers for Disease Control and Prevention to study health care issues tried to understand the effect of gun control laws on shooting deaths nationwide each year.

Evidence Is Inconclusive

The panel examined 51 studies that attempted to determine if a specific law or combination of laws had any impact on violent crime. The review covered widely published academic studies that both support gun control and those concluding the laws are misguided.

Last October [2003] the task force released its report, saying there is "insufficient evidence to draw conclusions" about whether licensing, registering or banning firearms accomplishes the goal of reducing gun violence. It also pointedly said its finding should not be construed as proof the laws do not work—the panel simply could not say either way.

The CDC panel's report highlights what has come to be one of the more frustrating hurdles in the gun control debate: Many of the studies are scientifically unsound, incomplete or contradictory.

"A lot of the research that's done . . . is sort of research in name only and it's done by partisan groups," said Alan Lizotte, a University of Albany criminologist who teaches a graduate course on gun control.

The assault weapons ban that expired Sept. 13 [2004] covered the manufacture, sale and possession of nearly two dozen semiautomatic rifles and pistols. Its demise prompted a rash of dire predictions from gun control advocates who warn of coming violence.

"My leadership is playing Russian roulette," U.S. Rep. Christopher Shays, R-Conn., said. "There will be without question a horrific crime committed without an assault weapon ban, and every member of Congress will have to ask where were they on this issue."

Yet even proponents of the ban have acknowledged that it did little to reduce violent crime.

In a March [2004] interview with National Public Radio, Tom Diaz, a senior policy analyst with the Violence Policy Center, said, "If the existing assault weapons ban expires, I personally do not believe it will make one whit of difference one way or another in terms of our objective, which is reducing death and injury and getting a particularly lethal class of firearms off the streets."

Diaz's Washington-based organization, which bills itself as "the most aggressive group in the gun control movement," later backed away from his statement and fought hard for the law's renewal. It later released a statement saying the ban did little because the gun industry "made a mockery" of its loopholes by simply making cosmetic changes that did nothing to change the lethality of the guns.

"The only difference is that the arbitrary distinction between pre- and post-ban assault weapons is now gone," the group said.

Conceived and passed at a time when drug-fueled gun crime soared to record levels and several high-profile mass shootings horrified the country, the ban's supporters hoped it would keep criminals from getting their hands on weapons they believed to be particularly useful for mass killing.

But opponents, led by the 4 million-member National Rifle Association [NRA], called it a smoke screen to hide movement toward a more comprehensive gun ban.

"It's a bad policy and none of it has anything to do with the NRA and all of it has to do with common sense," Andrew Arulanandam, NRA director of public affairs, said in a telephone interview from the association's national headquarters in Fairfax, Va. Arulanandam said the law missed its target by focusing on guns seldom used in crimes and by assuming criminals would obey the law.

Cutting through the rhetoric, researchers initially commissioned by the Justice Department during the [Bill] Clinton administration concluded in July that "the ban's impact on gun violence is likely to be small at best."

"We cannot clearly credit the ban with any of the nation's recent drop in gun violence," wrote the report's authors, criminologists at the University of Pennsylvania.

The researchers noted the banned guns were used in only about 6 percent of all gun crimes before the law went into effect. Use of the banned weapons fell to about 1.7 percent of all gun crimes.

Enforcing the Law Should Be a Priority

Nationwide, firearms-related deaths dropped 25 percent between 1993 and 2001 and all gun crime fell by 63 percent. Because assault weapons are a small share of the market, some researchers attribute that precipitous drop to a number of factors, including tougher enforcement of existing laws, rather than the ban.

What's more, criminals simply used other kinds of guns, said the report, which came out after the CDC review of research on gun control.

"To me that symbolizes pretty well the nature of the gun control debate," said Robert J. Spitzer, a State University College at Cortland political science professor and author of the book, "The Politics of Gun Control."

The ban, Spitzer said, only escaped Congress because it was so weak.

"The very fact that it was enacted at all was a miracle," he said of the ban, which passed the House of Representatives by just two votes. "But if you look at it objectively, its impact has been pretty marginal."

Mike Spenello is a bartender of sorts for New York gun owners. They come into his shop, lean on the counter and spill their frustrations.

"It's the criminal element that's making it hard for us to keep our guns," said Spenello, who works the counter at Taylor and Vadney Sporting Goods in Rotterdam. It's something he and his customers have been saying for years: Laws that restrict law-abiding citizens do little to reduce gun violence.

"Anybody who wants to commit a crime is not going to go through the process of getting a permit. There's a paper trail three miles long," said Spenello, who won't even allow a prospective customer to touch a handgun at the counter without first showing a permit.

There are no concrete statistics about how often any of New York state's roughly 1.2 million licensed handgun owners commit a gun crime. Still, authorities say it is extremely rare.

"You could count them on one hand in a year," said retired State Police Lt. Lee O. Thomas, who in the 1970s ran the State Police's Pistol Permit Bureau, which is a repository for the county-issued licenses. Thomas and Chamberlain, the former counsel, co-authored "Gun Control in New York," which details the nuances of state gun laws.

Most Gun Crimes Involve Handguns

Criminals, meanwhile, were still able to obtain the guns used in 14,659 serious gun crimes in New York state in 2001, the most recent year of complete data maintained by the state Division of Criminal Justice Services. About 86 percent of those guns were handguns—the most heavily regulated type of firearm in the state.

"That's proof that somehow the law has failed," said Spenello, echoing the feelings of many gun owners.

Spenello nonetheless supports some sort of screening of gun buyers. He said policy-makers should focus on how criminals get guns, not on guns seldom used in crimes or gun owners who are no danger to society.

Many criminologists are quick to point out that the public's concept of the danger posed by guns is drastically distorted.

Violent crime often receives dramatic coverage in the media, leading to a feeling that gun violence is epidemic. But violent crime rates and murder rates, considered by experts to be the most reliable crime statistic, are down in New York and nationwide.

New York state's murder rate has dropped about 50 percent since the early 1970s and is nearly identical to the rate in 1965. More recently, murders have dropped 64 percent since the height of inner-city drug violence in the early 1990s, with violent crime down 54 percent.

So if the link between gun control laws and gun crime is as tenuous as many criminologists and policy-makers believe, then why do both sides in the debate devote so much time, energy and money arguing about it?

Spitzer, the Cortland professor, said the seemingly endless debate is fueled by politics, paranoia, propaganda and ignorance from both sides.

"The gun control debate itself is not particularly rational," he said.

CHAPTER 2

The Causes of Gun Violence

Media Violence Is Linked to Aggressive Behavior

Media Awareness Network

The following viewpoint surveys many studies that have found links between media violence and acts of aggression. While the evidence remains inconclusive, consistent exposure to violence may impact behavior. The Media Awareness Network is a Canadian not-for-profit center for media education.

Whether or not exposure to media violence causes increased levels of aggression and violence in young people is the perennial question of media effects research. Some experts, like University of Michigan professor L. Rowell Huesmann, argue that fifty years of evidence show "that exposure to media violence causes children to behave more aggressively and affects them as adults years later." Others, like Jonathan Freedman of the University of Toronto, maintain that "the scientific evidence simply does not show that watching violence either produces violence in people, or desensitizes them to it."

Many Studies, Many Conclusions

Andrea Martinez at the University of Ottawa conducted a comprehensive review of the scientific literature for the Canadian Radio-television and Telecommunications Commission (CRTC) in 1994. She concluded that the lack of consensus about media effects reflects three "grey areas" or constraints contained in the research itself.

First, media violence is notoriously hard to define and measure. Some experts who track violence in television pro-

Media Awareness Network, "Research on the Effects of Media Violence," MediaAwarenessNetwork.com, September 22, 2007. © 2008 Media Awareness Network, www.media-awareness.ca, adapted with permission.

gramming, such as George Gerbner of Temple University, define violence as the act (or threat) of injuring or killing someone, independent of the method used or the surrounding context. Accordingly, Gerbner includes cartoon violence in his data-set. But others, such as University of Laval professors Guy Paquette and Jacques de Guise, specifically exclude cartoon violence from their research because of its comical and unrealistic presentation.

Second, researchers disagree over the type of relationship the data supports. Some argue that exposure to media violence causes aggression. Others say that the two are associated, but that there is no causal connection. (That both, for instance, may be caused by some third factor.) And others say the data supports the conclusion that there is no relationship between the two at all.

Third, even those who agree that there is a connection between media violence and aggression disagree about how the one effects the other. Some say that the mechanism is a psychological one, rooted in the ways we learn. For example, Huesmann argues that children develop "cognitive scripts" that guide their own behaviour by imitating the actions of media heroes. As they watch violent shows, children learn to internalize scripts that use violence as an appropriate method of problem-solving.

Media Violence Has Effect in Real Life

Others researchers argue that it is the physiological effects of media violence that cause aggressive behaviour. Exposure to violent imagery is linked to increased heart rate, faster respiration and higher blood pressure. Some think that this simulated "fight-or-flight" response predisposes people to act aggressively in the real world.

Still others focus on the ways in which media violence primes or cues pre-existing aggressive thoughts and feelings. They argue that an individual's desire to strike out is justified by media images in which both the hero and the villain use violence to seek revenge, often without consequences.

In her final report to the CRTC, Martinez concluded that most studies support "a positive, though weak, relation between exposure to television violence and aggressive behaviour." Although that relationship cannot be "confirmed systematically," she agrees with Dutch researcher Tom Van der Voot who argues that it would be illogical to conclude that "a phenomenon does not exist simply because it is found at times not to occur, or only to occur under certain circumstances."

The lack of consensus about the relationship between media violence and real-world aggression has not impeded ongoing research. Here's a sampling of conclusions drawn to date, from the various research strands:

Research strand: Children who consume high levels of media violence are more likely to be aggressive in the real world.

In 1956, researchers took to the laboratory to compare the behaviour of 24 children watching TV. Half watched a violent episode of the cartoon *Woody Woodpecker*, and the other 12 watched the non-violent cartoon *The Little Red Hen*. During play afterwards, the researchers observed that the children who watched the violent cartoon were much more likely to hit other children and break toys.

Six years later, in 1963, professors A. Badura, D. Ross and S.A. Ross studied the effect of exposure to real-world violence, television violence, and cartoon violence. They divided 100 preschool children into four groups. The first group watched a real person shout insults at an inflatable doll while hitting it with a mallet. The second group watched the incident on television. The third watched a cartoon version of the same scene, and the fourth watched nothing.

Media-Learned Aggression

When all the children were exposed to a frustrating situation, the first three groups responded with more aggression than the control group. The children who watched the incident on television were just as aggressive as those who had watched the real person use the mallet; and both were more aggressive than those who had only watched the cartoon.

Over the years, laboratory experiments such as these have consistently shown that exposure to violence is associated with increased heartbeat, blood pressure and respiration rate, and a greater willingness to administer electric shocks to inflict pain or punishment on others. However, this line of enquiry has been criticized because of its focus on short-term results and the artificial nature of the viewing environment.

Other scientists have sought to establish a connection between media violence and aggression outside the laboratory. For example, a number of surveys indicate that children and young people who report a preference for violent entertainment also score higher on aggression indexes than those who watch less violent shows. L. Rowell Huesmann reviewed studies conducted in Australia, Finland, Poland, Israel, Netherlands and the United States. He reports, "the child most likely to be aggressive would be the one who (a) watches violent television programs most of the time, (b) believes that these shows portray life just as it is, [and] (c) identifies strongly with the aggressive characters in the shows."

Imitation of Behaviours

A study conducted by the Kaiser Family Foundation in 2003 found that nearly half (47 per cent) of parents with children between the ages of 4 and 6 report that their children have imitated aggressive behaviours from TV. However, it is interesting to note that children are more likely to mimic positive behaviours—87 per cent of kids do so.

Recent research is exploring the effect of new media on children's behaviour. Craig Anderson and Brad Bushman of Iowa State University reviewed dozens of studies of video gamers. In 2001, they reported that children and young people who play violent video games, even for short periods, are more likely to behave aggressively in the real world; and that both aggressive and non-aggressive children are negatively affected by playing.

In 2003, Craig Anderson and Iowa State University colleague Nicholas Carnagey and Janie Eubanks of the Texas Department of Human Services reported that violent music lyrics increased aggressive thoughts and hostile feelings among 500 college students. They concluded, "There are now good theoretical and empirical reasons to expect effects of music lyrics on aggressive behavior to be similar to the well-studied effects of exposure to TV and movie violence and the more recent research efforts on violent video games."

Research Strand: Children who watch high levels of media violence are at increased risk of aggressive behaviour as adults.

In 1960, University of Michigan professor Leonard Eron studied 856 grade three students living in a semi-rural community in Columbia County, New York, and found that the children who watched violent television at home behaved more aggressively in school. Eron wanted to track the effect of this exposure over the years, so he revisited Columbia County in 1971, when the children who participated in the 1960 study were 19 years of age. He found that boys who watched violent TV when they were eight were more likely to get in trouble with the law as teenagers.

A Chain of Aggression

When Eron and Huesmann returned to Columbia County in 1982, the subjects were 30 years old. They reported that those participants who had watched more violent TV as eight-year-olds were more likely, as adults, to be convicted of serious crimes, to use violence to discipline their children, and to treat their spouses aggressively.

Professor Monroe Lefkowitz published similar findings in 1971. Lefkowitz interviewed a group of eight-year-olds and found that the boys who watched more violent TV were more likely to act aggressively in the real world. When he interviewed the same boys ten years later, he found that the more violence a boy watched at eight, the more aggressively he would act at age eighteen.

Columbia University professor Jeffrey Johnson has found that the effect is not limited to violent shows. Johnson tracked 707 families in upstate New York for 17 years, starting in 1975. In 2002, Johnson reported that children who watched one to three hours of television each day when they were 14 to 16 years old were 60 per cent more likely to be involved in assaults and fights as adults than those who watched less TV.

Kansas State University professor John Murray concludes, "The most plausible interpretation of this pattern of correlations is that early preference for violent television programming and other media is one factor in the production of aggressive and antisocial behavior when the young boy becomes a young man."

However, this line of research has attracted a great deal of controversy. Pulitzer Prize–winning author Richard Rhodes has attacked Eron's work, arguing that his conclusions are based on an insignificant amount of data. Rhodes claims that Eron had information about the amount of TV viewed in 1960 for only 3 of the 24 men who committed violent crimes as adults years later. Rhodes concludes that Eron's work is "poorly conceived, scientifically inadequate, biased and sloppy if not actually fraudulent research."

Guy Cumberbatch, head of the Communications Research Group, a U.K. social policy think tank, has equally harsh words for Johnson's study. Cumberbatch claims Johnson's group of 88 under-one-hour TV watchers is "so small, it's aberrant." And, as journalist Ben Shouse points out, other critics say that Johnson's study "can't rule out the possibility that television is just a marker for some unmeasured environmental or psychological influence on both aggression and TV habits."

Research Strand: The introduction of television into a community leads to an increase in violent behaviour.

Researchers have also pursued the link between media violence and real life aggression by examining communities before and after the introduction of television. In the mid 1970s, University of British Columbia professor Tannis McBeth Williams studied a remote village in British Columbia both before and after television was introduced. She found that two years after TV arrived, violent incidents had increased by 160 per cent.

Researchers Gary Granzberg and Jack Steinbring studied three Cree [an indigenous people of North America] communities in northern Manitoba during the 1970s and early 1980s. They found that four years after television was introduced into one of the communities, the incidence of fist fights and black eyes among the children had increased significantly. Interestingly, several days after an episode of *Happy Days* aired, in which one character joined a gang called the Red Demons, children in the community created rival gangs, called the Red Demons and the Green Demons, and the conflict between the two seriously disrupted the local school.

Links Between TV and Crime

University of Washington professor Brandon Centerwall noted that the sharp increase in the murder rate in North America in 1955 occurred eight years after television sets began to enter North American homes. To test his hypothesis that the two were related, he examined the murder rate in South Africa where, prior to 1975, television was banned by the government. He found that twelve years after the ban was lifted, murder rates skyrocketed.

University of Toronto professor Jonathan Freedman has criticized this line of research. He points out that Japanese television has some of the most violent imagery in the world, and yet Japan has a much lower murder rate than other countries, including Canada and the United States, which have comparatively less violence on TV.

Research Strand: Media violence stimulates fear in some children.

A number of studies have reported that watching media violence frightens young children, and that the effects of this may be long lasting.

In 1998, Professors Singer, Slovak, Frierson and York surveyed 2,000 Ohio students in grades three through eight. They report that the incidences of psychological trauma (including anxiety, depression and post-traumatic stress) increased in proportion to the number of hours of television watched each day. . . .

Research Strand: Media violence desensitizes people to real violence.

A number of studies in the 1970's showed that people who are repeatedly exposed to media violence tend to be less disturbed when they witness real world violence, and have less sympathy for its victims. For example, Professors V.B. Cline, R.G. Croft, and S. Courrier studied young boys over a two-year period. In 1973, they reported that boys who watch more than 25 hours of television per week are significantly less likely to be aroused by real world violence than those boys who watch 4 hours or less per week.

When researchers Fred Molitor and Ken Hirsch revisited this line of investigation in 1994, their work confirmed that children are more likely to tolerate aggressive behaviour in the real world if they first watch TV shows or films that contain violent content.

Research Strand: People who watch a lot of media violence tend to believe that the world is more dangerous than it is in reality.

George Gerbner has conducted the longest running study of television violence. His seminal research suggests that heavy TV viewers tend to perceive the world in ways that are consistent with the images on TV. As viewers' perceptions of the world come to conform with the depictions they see on TV, they become more passive, more anxious, and more fearful. Gerbner calls this the "Mean World Syndrome."

Gerbner's research found that those who watch greater amounts of television are more likely to

- overestimate their risk of being victimized by crime;

- believe their neighbourhoods are unsafe;

- believe "fear of crime is a very serious personal problem;"

- assume the crime rate is increasing, even when it is not.

André Gosselin, Jacques de Guise and Guy Paquette decided to test Gerbner's theory in the Canadian context in 1997. They surveyed 360 university students, and found that heavy television viewers are more likely to believe the world is a more dangerous place. However, they also found heavy viewers are not more likely to actually feel more fearful.

Research Strand: Family attitudes to violent content are more important than the images themselves.

A number of studies suggest that media is only one of a number of variables that put children at risk of aggressive behaviour.

For example, a Norwegian study that included 20 at-risk teenaged boys found that the lack of parental rules regulating what the boys watched was a more significant predictor of aggressive behaviour than the amount of media violence they watched. It also indicated that exposure to real world violence, together with exposure to media violence, created an "overload" of violent events. Boys who experienced this overload were more likely to use violent media images to create and consolidate their identities as members of an anti-social and marginalized group.

On the other hand, researchers report that parental attitudes towards media violence can mitigate the impact it has on children. Huesmann and Bacharach conclude, "Family attitudes and social class are stronger determinants of attitudes toward aggression than is the amount of exposure to TV, which is nevertheless a significant but weaker predictor."

Guns Protect People

Sharon Harris

Giving many examples from real-life incidents, the author of the following viewpoint argues that the right to bear arms protects the individual from violent aggressors and from the ineffective protection state and federal government is offering its citizens. She contends that only criminals benefit from gun control laws that make it more difficult for ordinary citizens to protect themselves. Sharon Harris is president of the Advocates for Self-Government, a nonprofit nonpartisan libertarian educational organization.

On May 11, 1993, Justin Dey's nightmare is about to begin. The 19-year-old young man is alone in his Atlanta home. Suddenly there's a loud pounding on the front door. He peeks out the window. He sees two strangers in his front yard, one staring at the house, the other pounding on the door. The house had been broken into three times in recent months.

So, terrified, Justin grabs the phone and dials 911. But even as he's talking to the police, the strange men enter the fenced backyard. They begin kicking against the back door. The wood starts to splinter. "They're coming in!" Justin shouts into the phone. He grabs a handgun his father gave him after the last break in. The door smashes open. As the men enter, Justin raises the gun and fires. He kills the first intruder, the other two flee.

We continue to hear about the evils of gun ownership. Especially with the tragic school shootings, there has been a lot of demonization of guns and gun owners. Guns are portrayed as tools of crime and murder, and gun ownership is portrayed as a detriment to society—a bad thing.

Sharon Harris, "What Should We Do About Guns?" Advocates for Self-Government, August 28, 2007. Copyright © 2007 Advocates for Self-Government. Reproduced by permission.

Guns Benefit Society

I disagree. I submit to you that not only are guns not evil, but that guns are a great benefit to our society. That's a view that's not heard very often, but is one that all Americans need to hear. That's why I want to talk to you about it today. In fact, what I'm about to share with you could save your life or the lives of your loved ones.

Let's go back to the story I began with. When young Justin used a gun to protect his life and property, he was hardly unique. In fact, leading criminologist Gary Kleck—who incidentally is a liberal Democrat and an ACLU [American Civil Liberties Union] member—found that American gun owners use their guns almost 2.5 million times per year to ward off criminal attack. That's once every 13 seconds! That means that since I started speaking, 8 times Americans have used guns to protect themselves.

Most of the time, the guns are not even fired. Just showing a gun is enough to send criminals fleeing. Without guns, homeowners and their families would be at the mercy of murderers, rapists, burglars, and other thugs. Guns provide even the weak and elderly the ability to defend themselves against crime. In fact, we could say handguns are a girl's best friend. When we think about the violence and threats of violence that are out there, diamonds just don't cut it.

They don't call guns "equalizers" for nothing.

Guns Offer Protection

Increasingly, women are becoming aware of this and are more than ever turning to handguns for protection.

Anti-gun forces don't like this. They say this is a bad idea.

Peter Shields, founder of Handgun Control Inc.—the largest gun control group in America—has some advice for women threatened by attackers. He says, "Give them what they want." As a woman, mother and grandmother, I find this highly offensive.

The anti-gun forces also tell women it's dangerous to carry a gun or try to use it against an attacker, because, they say, the attacker is likely to seize the gun and turn it against the woman. You've all heard that argument, right? Well, it's simply not true.

According to liberal criminologist Don Cates, there is no recorded example anywhere of an armed woman having her gun seized by a rapist and used against her. Let me repeat that: there is no recorded example anywhere of an armed woman having her gun seized by a rapist and used against her.

Even more amazing, the government's own Bureau of Justice Statistics found that criminals were able to turn guns against their owners—male or female—in less than 1% of cases.

Armed Resistance Is Effective

And the anti-gun argument that it's dangerous to resist a criminal attack is simply wrong. Criminologist Kleck studied U.S. Justice Department figures and found that "for both robbery and assault, victims who used guns for protection were less likely either to be attacked or injured than victims that responded in any other way, including those who did not resist at all."

Furthermore, the best research shows that rape attempts against women who are armed almost always fail. The failure rate is around 98%!

Maybe guns *ARE* a girl's best friend.

There's no doubt that guns are a major way for women, for the weak, for smaller people, the elderly—anyone who may be vulnerable, *NOT* to be weak and vulnerable.

Bottom line: guns protect people.

Another way that guns are a blessing is one simple and seemingly obvious fact: criminals are afraid of guns. That's not just a guess, either. Research bears this out, and it's a very important point.

A three-year study by the National Institute of Justice surveyed 1,800 convicted felons and confirmed that criminals strongly fear meeting armed resistance by potential victims. Fully 74% said they believe burglars avoid houses where people are at home because they're afraid they'll get shot; 39% said they personally had called a halt to a particular planned crime because they feared the victim might be armed. The study also found that felons from states with high gun ownership worried the most about being shot.

This seems like common sense—that criminals are afraid of guns. But when it comes to discussion of this issue, many people throw common sense out the window.

A Gun for Every Home

Here's a virtual lab experiment that shows the truth of this research. Kennesaw, GA, near where I live, in 1981 passed a law requiring all households to have a gun. The law received worldwide coverage, with many people laughing about it and some predicting a blood bath. After all, if gun ownership led to death and violence, surely the town would be covered in blood, right? Seven years later, although the population had almost doubled, annual home burglaries had dropped from 11 per 1,000 houses to 2.6 per 1,000 houses—a 400% decrease in burglaries in the fastest-growing town. . . . Kennesaw still has that law and the low crime rates continue.

This isn't just recent. Let's go back to 1966. In that year, the number of rapes in Orlando, FL tripled—and that was accompanied by a dramatic increase in robberies as well. This terrified the community—particularly women. Police began offering well-publicized courses in how to use handguns, and over 2500 women promptly took the course. Apparently, word got out to criminals and would-be criminals that women had guns and knew how to use them. One year later, the rape, assault, robbery and burglary rate had all plummeted in Orlando, while over the rest of the state they continued to rise.

This same thing has happened in many other communities.

The fact that guns deter crimes—millions of them a year—has been proven over and over again—by anecdotes, by examples like Kennesaw and Orlando, and by the best research by the best criminologists in America.

Guns save lives and gun ownership is a great benefit to America.

I want to give you one more example of cutting-edge research that I found amazing.

Research Finds That Guns Prevent Crime

In the largest study of its type ever done, Dr. John Lott and David Mustard of the University of Chicago examined crime statistics in every single county in the U.S. from 1977 to 1992. They found abundant, unequivocal evidence that gun ownership is a major deterrence to violence. In the 31 states that have "shall issue" laws—where any adult without criminal records or evidence of mental illness is permitted to carry a concealed gun—crime rates are far lower than in states where there are no such laws. Their research shows that, using the most conservative estimates, those states reduced their murder rate by an average of 8.5%, rapes by 5%, aggravated assaults by 7% and robbery by 3%.

Those statistics have human faces. According to Lott and Mustard, if the states that didn't have "shall issue" laws had instead adopted them in 1992, the country would have been spared 12,000 robberies, 60,000 aggravated assaults, 4,177 rapes and 1,570 murders—per year.

Here's a real-life example of lives that could have been saved.

A few years ago there was a well-publicized mass shooting at a McDonald's. One woman who was in the restaurant when it happened had left her handgun in the car—because her state had no "shall issue" laws. If she had had her gun with her, she could have saved several lives—including those of her mother and father whom she watched gunned down.

Again, the fact that guns deter crimes—millions of them a year—has been proven over and over again.

In spite of all these facts, today we're seeing more and more calls for gun control. . . .

The Second Amendment Is in Danger

This is a disturbing trend. During the past few years, we've seen a New York congressman introduce legislation to entirely abolish the 2nd Amendment. We've seen Sen. John Chaffe—a powerful Republican Senator from RI—propose legislation that would totally outlaw private ownership of handguns and require all citizens to turn over their handguns to the government. If you fail to turn over your gun, you would be fined $5,000 and sentenced to up to 5 years in prison. Even conservative columnist George Will has called for getting rid of the 2nd Amendment.

Of course most proposals are far less dramatic. Some of the proposals sound very reasonable. Like a waiting period. Makes sense, right? Let the person cool down a little. But remember the Los Angeles riots? Here was a situation where innocent, law-abiding, peaceful citizens found their homes, businesses, families and lives threatened by unbridled violence. Many of them had never even thought of having a gun, but now they needed one. When they tried to get guns, they had a rude awakening: in Los Angeles there is a 14-day waiting period. Suddenly that 14-day waiting period didn't seem so reasonable anymore.

And consider Katherine Latte, a mail carrier in Charlotte, NC. Her ex-boyfriend had robbed her and raped her, and she feared he might kill her. She went down to apply for a gun and was informed that there'd be a 2–4 week waiting period. "I'll be dead by then," she told authorities, to no avail. So she bought an illegal gun for $20 on the street. Five hours later, her ex-boyfriend attacked her outside her house and she shot him dead.

A Wisconsin woman was not so lucky. She had a restraining order against her husband who had threatened her and her children. She called a firearms instructor to inquire about getting a gun and was told there'd be a 48-hour waiting period. Just 48 hours. Sounds pretty reasonable, huh? Well, 24 hours later she and her children were dead.

Waiting periods sound very reasonable in legislative chambers. But not so reasonable in real life.

Women Need Protection

It's because of stories like these—and there's no end to them— that I agree with prominent female gun rights advocate Sonny Jones, who fears that proposed laws will keep women from getting much-needed weapons. She says, "I do not approve of background checks, waiting periods, registration, or mandatory training. It is our right to use whatever means we choose to protect ourselves. We have nothing to prove, we need no one's permission."

Another reason I fear seemingly reasonable gun control proposals is that I believe there is a hidden agenda behind many of them. And that is the banning and confiscation of firearms in America. This is not just paranoia. Peter Shields, founder of Handgun Control Inc., the country's biggest gun-control organization, now headed by Sarah Brady, the people who brought you the Brady Bill—let the cat out of the bag. In 1976, he wrote in the *New Yorker* that the organization's "ultimate goal" was "to make the possession of all handguns and all handgun ammunition except for the military, policemen, licensed security guards, licensed sporting clubs, and licensed gun collectors—totally illegal."

Does this sound implausible? Well, it's happened recently in Britain and in Australia. Similar broad bans are being introduced in state legislatures across America. If some of the anti-gun forces have their way, America is next.

Gun Control Only Benefits Criminals

To some of you, this may even sound like a good idea. Let's get rid of guns, and then we won't have violence. But it doesn't work that way. Keep in mind that all proposals to ban guns are aimed at law-abiding, non-violent citizens. Criminals—who by definition ignore laws against burglary, rape, assault, murder—will also disregard laws against guns.

Whatever the anti-gun lobby tells you, the truth is that every year guns save the lives of huge numbers of children and adults—far more lives than are lost to gun violence or accidents.

The truth is that violent crime has been dropping every year since 1991.

The truth is that none of the recent shootings were done with legal guns.

The truth is gun control disarms law-abiding citizens, not criminals.

The truth is that if a criminal knows he may be met with a gun, he is far less likely to violate a home or commit an assault.

I hope you're convinced that guns are actually a benefit to society.

But as important as guns are in fighting crime and saving lives, that's not the main reason I support the right to bear arms. As a libertarian, the main reason I support this vital right is for the same reason that the Founding Fathers did. It was not for hunting furry little animals or Bambi's Mom. It wasn't even for protection against crime or to make sure we could defend our borders. It was because they knew that, throughout history, the greatest threat to life and liberty has always come from government—and they believed that an armed citizenry would be the best protection against government tyranny developing in America.

All the stories you hear from history—around the world—about ethnic cleansing, oppression of minorities, totalitarian regimes—none of these could have happened if the people were armed.

The Second Amendment is the "enforcement clause" of the rest of the Bill of Rights. The right to keep and bear arms is, like free speech and religious freedom, a central part of our political heritage as a free people. We *must* preserve it.

Very Young Perpetrators Are Victims of Gun Accessibility

Family Education Network

This viewpoint explains the dangers of bringing guns into families' homes. Guns are desirable objects for children—especially boys—and if not locked up properly, they can become lethal. The safest environment for kids, the authors argue, is one without weapons. Launched in 1996 as the first parenting site on the Web, Family Education has become a site for those seeking information and advice on family and parenting issues.

The six-year-old boy who killed his six-year-old classmate at a Michigan elementary school is perceived by many as the youngest child to kill someone with a firearm. But he's not even close.

If we put aside the multitude of young kids who shoot other young kids accidentally (with guns that adults insisted were too high up or too well-hidden to be found by such small kids), we're confronted with the sad reality of children who shoot others intentionally. But whether kids kill because they've accidentally misfired a gun or because they intended to murder schoolmates or family members, we're still faced with the same troubling question: Why did the child have access to a gun in the first place?

Why They Do It

That many young killers target people in their own families—often abusive fathers and stepfathers—no longer comes as a surprise. But what's still shocking is that some of these kids are so young.

Family Education Network, "Why Little Kids Kill," FamilyEducation.com, August 27, 2007. Copyright © 2007 Pearson Education, Inc. All rights reserved. Reproduced by permission of Pearson Education, Inc.

A boy I'll call Robbie shot and killed his father after watching his mother being beaten. His drunken father had left a gun on the table and though Robbie confessed to the killing, few people initially believed that he could have done it. That's because he was only *three years old*. After gunpowder tests confirmed him as the killer, he explained to authorities: "I killed him. Now he's dead. If he would have hit my mother again, I would have shot him again."

Drew Golden was just 11 years old when he and another boy shot 15 people in Jonesboro, Arkansas. Santa gave Drew a shotgun when he was 6. He was taught to hunt as a tot and later perfected his reflexes with violent video games. When Drew wanted guns for his shooting spree, he got them where almost all young killers get their guns: home. To his credit, Drew's father had a gun vault the boys couldn't open; to his discredit, the boys were still able to find 3 unsecured handguns. They got 7 more guns from the home of Drew's grandfather.

Boys Will Be Boys

Guns give tragic permanence to hostilities and disagreements that would otherwise pass with time. Though the NRA [National Rifle Association] and other gun advocates claim the solutions to the gun-violence crisis are education and training, boys cannot be taught to be adults. Boys have poor impulse control; they are immature and adventurous. They are, in short, boys. Few parents would leave a blowtorch or dynamite around the house for an unsupervised boy to play with, yet many parents allow access to guns, either intentionally or negligently.

We don't let boys drive, buy alcohol or cigarettes, vote, or get married, but many parents provide them access to guns. Almost a decade ago, the *Journal of the American Medical Association* reported that 1.2 million elementary-aged latchkey kids had access to guns in the home. Given that 20,000 guns enter the stream of commerce each day, that figure is even worse today.

Gun Lust

A simple fact of the species is that boys and men love guns. Shot from the back porch at some tin cans or shot from an aircraft carrier at some Iraqi soldiers, it's no matter—we can't get enough of them.

So while you may be able to keep your son from owning a gun, if you try to talk him out of wanting one, you are up against a pretty strong argument: *You mean I shouldn't want a device that grants me power and identity, makes me feel dangerous and safe at the same time, instantly makes me the dominant male, and connects me to my evolutionary essence? Come on, Mom, get real!*

And when he enters his teens, a million cells swimming in testosterone will stir mysterious male cravings that holler: "Dominate!"—because that's how you get the good chicks. So are we curious about guns? Curiosity doesn't touch it—we are enraptured. On the news, on TV—on a shelf in the attic. In a movie, in a toy store—in Mom or Dad's bedside drawer. In a magazine, in a video game, in a friend's house—just try to keep it from us.

Guns Are Desirable

Some boys go through a gun phase we could call a brief fling; others marry the gun for life. Whatever path your son ultimately takes, he'll need to have a clear understanding of your policies about firearms, as well as the consequences of violating those policies. That means parents have to make some decisions:

- Do we want to have a gun in the house?

- If so, where do we want to keep it?

- How do we want to store it?

- How do we want to secure it?

- Do we want it to be a secret from the kids?

- Do we want to teach our kids how to use a gun?

- Do we want to give our son a gun of his own?

Gun owners need to keep guns locked; that's an easy one. The question of whether to keep the location of a gun secret from a child is also easy: You may elect to treat it as a secret, but never, ever rely upon the belief that a child cannot find a gun in the house.

Tamper-Proof Weapons?

Guns could have components that inhibit firing by children, or technologies that allow operation only in the hands of the owner (with a coded ring or wristband, for example). But today, it's easier to shoot most handguns than it is to open a bottle of children's vitamins.

Speaking of tamper-proof containers, the design of billions of bottles of consumer products was changed after the deaths of 8 people from poisoned Tylenol—tragedy completely beyond the control of the manufacturer. Gun-makers, on the other hand, knowingly and enthusiastically build products that *kill 500 Americans each week*, and we don't require a single safety feature.

Consider this: There are four categories of federal safety regulations covering the manufacture of teddy bears, but none about guns. Today, firearms are unique among consumer goods in America in that they are not governed by any federal safety regulations. While most every business is concerned with delivering its product or service safely, gun manufacturers are studying ways to make their products more lethal. They work to make them more portable, more rapid, and more effective at damaging human tissue. And the more high-tech guns become, the more crucial it is for us to address the gun access issue.

Keep Your Kids Safe

Some gun owners explain that they needn't lock their weapons because they don't have children. To them I say: Other people do have children, and they will visit your home one day. The plumber who answers your weekend emergency will bring along his bored nine-year-old son, and that boy will find your gun.

In the meantime, if you own a gun, or you know someone who does, make sure that the gun itself—not just the cabinet, closet, or drawer that you store it in—is kept locked. Doing this is the opposite of government gun control; it is *personal* gun control.

It's not even enough to be vigilant about the danger posed by guns in your own home. Whenever your kids visit or sleep over at someone else's house, always ask the supervising adult if there are guns in the house. A.S.K.: Asking Saves Kids.

Considering that so many parents make the choice to keep a gun in their homes, it's no wonder the rate of firearms deaths for young people in America is 12 times higher than in all the other industrialized countries—*combined.*

Thankfully, we all have the right to not bear arms; you can choose to make your home a weapons-free environment.

The United States Has a Cultural Obsession with Guns

Mark Morford

Using humor, the author of the following viewpoint takes on gun lobbyists and their main argument, that guns make the United States safer. He laments weak gun control laws and envisions a society that can give up one of its most revered pastimes to make the country safer for all. Mark Morford is a writer for SFGate-.com and the San Francisco Chronicle.

You know what offers just tremendous amounts of pleasure? Shooting guns.

It's true. Shotguns, handguns, rifles, BB guns, squirt guns, you name it. Try it yourself: Just head out to a shooting range and have the gun boys yank you some clay pigeons and blast those things out of the sky and oh my God it's just a ridiculous barefaced thrill, a sense of godlike power, a rush of adrenaline to go along with a hot buzz of precision and concentration and the smell of gunpowder and much manly macho grunting.

I am not at all joking. I've done it. I've even enjoyed it, quite a bit. Sport shooting is an intense rush, a unique sort of pleasure, scary and powerful and deadly and fascinating and, in its deep, pure violence, rather beautiful. What's more, guns can be gorgeous pieces of precision engineering, sexy and brutal and often superbly made and so dumbly phallic and obviously homoerotic it makes the men of the NRA [National Rifle Association] tingle every night, secretly.

But let this be known: Guns are also, quite clearly, something that could exit the human experience entirely and we would, very simply, only be the better for it. Much, much better. Oh yes we would.

Mark Morford, "Everyone Should Get a Gun!" *San Francisco Chronicle*, April 20, 2007. Republished with permission of *San Francisco Chronicle*, conveyed through Copyright Clearance Center, Inc.

Gun Laws Are Too Weak

Look, it's easy enough to point out all the obvious gun-control arguments the brutal Virginia Tech [VT] massacre [a school shooting on April 16, 2007] slaps across the face of the pro-gun culture. Guns are far too easy to obtain. Gun fetishism is far too prevalent and glamorized and legitimized in the States. Guns are often easier to get hold of than a driver's license and we don't even perform instant background checks, and in places like Texas it's now easier than ever not only to own a gun, but the state's newly expanded gun laws mean it's A-OK to shoot and kill someone for pretty much looking at you sideways, and if you do, not only is it unlikely you will go to jail for it, many Texans will actually applaud.

But the truth is, these issues aren't really the point. And as many politicians—even Democrats—are already pointing out, new gun-control legislation in the wake of VT isn't exactly a priority, mostly due to the vicious power of the tiny-but-vocal gun lobby and especially given the faux-cowboy gun-lovin' warmonger who currently holds the White House veto stamp in his insolent little fist right now [that is, George W. Bush].

But even the obvious fact that no new gun-control laws are likely to emerge hasn't stopped the pro-gunners from tossing up what is easily my favorite pro-gun argument of all time, one that's popped back up on blogs and forums and in right-wing columns all over the Net in response to VT, like some sort of cute, thuggish mantra of happy cancerous violence.

It goes like this: If only more people had guns, no one would get shot. If only everyone was armed and everyone was packing heat and everyone knew everyone else could kill them at a moment's notice, why, no one would dare shoot each other for fear of getting killed themselves before they even had a chance to enjoy their own murderous rage.

In other words, the solution to the too-many-guns-too-easily problem? *Even more guns.*

More to the point: If the professors and students at Virginia Tech just so happened to carry their own swell Glock 9mm in their backpacks or in their purses just like insane sullen loner Cho Seung-Hui, maybe he would've been less likely to go on that rampage because, gosh golly, he'd surely know he'd be quickly shot dead by 100 trigger-ready students as soon as he fired the first shot. And what satisfaction is there in a brutal gun rampage if you don't get to kill more than a handful of kids? It's such perfectly insane logic, they should print it on the NRA brochure. Hell, maybe they do.

Pro-gun Arguments Defy Logic

I love this line of thinking. It's like bashing your own skull with a brick and calling it intellectual stimulation.

Hell, it worked great for the Cold War, didn't it? Every major nation enjoys a grudging, caveman-esque respect for each other's massive nuke stockpile and whoever can annihilate the world the most times over gets the most power and we all live happily ever after in a brutal, anxious, fear-based society, some juvenile vision of a macho Wild West that never really existed. Beautiful.

It doesn't matter how overtly reckless and idiotic the "let's arm everyone" argument is. What matters is millions actually believe it. What matters is how many people, especially many who make the laws of the land (or coerce and lobby those who do) still believe this is some sort of core, defining ethos of the United States and even the world. It is, you have to admit, one hell of a way to run a planet.

But it is not the only way.

Here is the flip-side argument. It is at once simple and obvious and makes a calm sort of moral sense, and it therefore is sneered at by every gun lover and bitter Second Amendment misinterpreter and NRA lobbyist in the land.

Guns Could Disappear

It goes like this: If all guns were banned outright tomorrow, or even if we took the strict British/Swedish approach and only allowed them for hunting and in highly controlled shooting clubs, well, guns would slowly but surely disappear from the popular culture. As a fetish, as a gang weapon, as some sort of bogus macho self-defense argument, as an obvious and too-easy means to shocking schoolyard massacre, guns and the fear-based culture they create would, slowly but surely, fizzle and die.

It would not be instantaneous. It would not be easy. But slowly, as manufacturing largely ceased and gun shows shut down and fewer and fewer new firearms entered the channel and the black market slowly dried up from lack of decent supply, and as the upcoming generation simply wouldn't know a world where guns were prevalent and easy and stupid as paint, well, guns and the numb ultraviolence they inspire would disappear within a single generation, maybe two.

I know, it would ruin the all-American fun of shooting. I realize a beloved American hobby would have to be replaced by, well, roughly 10 thousand other options. I know it would infuriate countless collectors and responsible gun owners who merely appreciate the craftsmanship, the gun-maker's art, the simple joy of shooting deadly weapons into controlled targets and who have zero urge to kill anything, ever. I know.

But, well, so what? Giving up such a rather hollow, morally indefensible, outdated pleasure seems a tiny price to pay for the end result of a dramatically less violent America, a less suspicious, reactionary worldview, a nation *not* shot through with an undercurrent of fear and blood-drenched headlines and childish notions of angry, armed retaliation.

Hell, we've done it before, with all sorts of other harsh social practices and beliefs that, we finally realized, served the soul of our species not at all and actually caused much deep harm. Slavery. Hangings. The slaughter of Indians. Monarchical rule. Chamber pots. Flamethrowers. Smoking on airplanes. Lack of women's suffrage. Eugenics [improvement of the human race through selective breeding].

Really, has the time not come for guns to exit the wary American dream? Can we not even imagine it?

CHAPTER 3

Personal Perspectives on Gun Violence

Gun Violence Turns a Mother into a Gun Control Activist

Donna Dees-Thomases

In this viewpoint, the author describes how a violent incident she heard about from friends and witnessed on television, hit so close to home that her attitude toward gun control changed quickly and decisively. Trying to get involved with gun control groups was only her first step toward organizing the Million Mom March in Washington. Donna Dees-Thomases is a public relations consultant.

If there is such a thing as a moment being ripe for a revolution, then I would have to say the summer of 1999 was about as fertile as a warren of rabbits. We're talking egg counts that would put [egg-producing] Perdue [Farms] to shame.

Up until then, I was not an activist. I was just a mom.

My family and I were spending that August much as we had spent the last five summers—vacationing on Fire Island, an idyllic 31-mile-long barrier island off the coast of Long Island that, culturally, seems to be stuck in a wonderful kind of 1950s time warp. And that's why we like it so much. Cars are banned on the island for most of the summer, and kids on bikes compete for sidewalk space with adults pulling groceries in little red wagons.

Life in our town of Seaview is like life in *Leave It to Beaver* land, and this summer was no different—even if it was one of the hottest, driest summers on record. I did not mind the drought. A drought meant our beach house guestrooms would be filled with friends who needed to flee the sizzling streets of New York City, and I loved having company, because the rest

Donna Dees-Thomases, *Looking For a Few Good Moms*. Emmaus, PA: Rodale, Inc., 2004. © 2004 by Donna Dees-Thomases. All rights reserved. Reproduced with permission of Kuhn Projects, as agents for the author.

of the year, we lived in an isolated, northern New Jersey suburb, in a beautiful home stuck way off-road, abutting a forest reservation. Other than the occasional lost hiker, rarely did anyone drop by. Like a lot of isolated, suburban moms with small kids, I relished the weekly playgroups where we moms would get together to discuss who was the "best" pediatrician, or which were the "best" schools, or whether or not we had been to the newest store at the Mall at Short Hills. In other words, what we talked about was Stepford mom stuff. Rarely would we talk about ourselves or "unsafe" subjects such as religion or politics. And never did we discuss the more taboo ones like the politics of guns in America. But all of this was about to change.

Violence Changed My Life

The afternoon of August 10 should have been no different than any other lazy beach day, but that day I got a call from Robin Sheer, one of my New Jersey playgroup moms. Robin's daughters Elizabeth and Claudia both attended the same Jewish Community Center nursery school as my two daughters, Lili and Phoebe, and so I assumed she was calling so we could catch up on the girls. But this wasn't a social call. "Are you watching CNN?" Robin asked, sounding frantic.

No, I wasn't. Nor did I want to. Since leaving my full-time job at *CBS News* years before, I had happily traded in [news anchors] Dan Rather and Connie Chung for Barney, Elmo, and Big Bird. I didn't feel the compulsive need to always be tuned in to an all-news channel waiting for the latest, breaking story about some horrible catastrophe—unless it had something to do with mindless trash, like the Monica Lewinsky [and President Bill Clinton] scandal. Then I was glued to the tube. Since I had had children, I found the news to be, frankly, too full of bad news.

And Robin was calling about bad news. A Jewish Community Center in California had just been shot up; the kids attending day camp there were injured, maybe even dead. I clicked on the TV, saw the hovering helicopters, and the *BREAKING NEWS* headline, and immediately thought, "What mother in her right mind wants to watch this stuff?" Then I turned the TV off. Before I hung up with Robin, I probably "thanked" her for calling, and then I went back to one of my preferred sources of news—the *National Enquirer*, or maybe it was the *New York Post*.

As on most summer weekday nights, I was on my own with the kids because Jeff stayed in New Jersey so he could be within easier commuting distance to his office in the city. I missed him on these nights, but the trade-off was that I got to have the TV remote control all to myself once I put the kids to bed. On this August night, I settled in to have a few laughs at *Seinfeld*, and then at 11:35 P.M., I began to channel surf backward looking for Dave [late-night host David Letterman]. The show was in repeat, but I liked to see what it felt like to watch Dave like a regular viewer instead of seeing him at 5:30 P.M., the time the show was usually taped. As I surfed backward through the channels, toward Channel 2, home of Dave and the *Late Show*, I stumbled onto Channel 7, home of Ted Koppel and *Nightline*. My remote finger froze.

The News Was Shocking

The entire program that night was devoted to what had happened in Granada Hills, California, that morning. The North Valley Jewish Community Center [JCC] there was stormed by a gunman while a summer day-camp program was in session. This was what Robin called about earlier in the day. It seems that this guy just marched into the place and started shooting. Ted Koppel had just introduced taped footage of terrified children being led out of and away from the center by armed police. Good Lord, I wondered, how will those kids ever recover from that? How will they ever sleep again, having watched their friends be shot full of bullets? My heart was in my throat as I watched that chain of children, hand in hand, being led to safety. Something was terribly wrong with this picture. This was no daisy chain of happy, innocent children who were blissfully unaware of the evil in the world, safe on the grounds of their camp—this was a string of survivors being led away from a death trap. And those children could have been mine.

I was immobilized with shock. I stayed with the program and watched in horror as the television camera zoomed out to show the powerful images of SWAT teams leading these preschoolers off to safety.

The program then cut to two law-enforcement officials, one from Vancouver, the other from Seattle, who tried to apply reason to this insanity. Handguns and assault weapons, they both said, were much too easy to get in this country, especially compared with Canada, where the laws are much stricter. The Vancouver policeman talked about how strict the gun laws are in Canada, unlike those in America, where they are loose, lax, and riddled with loopholes. . . .

Instead of going to bed after *Nightline*, I went online, and what I found there not only shocked me, it scared me. After entering the search words "gun control," I found myself wandering into chat room after chat room overflowing with viciously worded, hate-fueled diatribes from gun-loving "Americans" who happened to hate other Americans who were Asian, African-American, Jewish, Latino, and, in some cases, women. The only thing they appeared to love more than their guns was making a profit by selling guns to other gun nuts like themselves. There was a lot of hate poorly camouflaged as patriotism in those chat rooms. It made me want to find an American flag and give it a good cleaning. Fast.

Gun Control Is Everybody's Problem

Apparently, events like the tragedy of Granada Hills prompted these gun nuts to come out of hiding and log on. I read the words of kids paying homage to Eric Harris and Dylan Klebold, the two teenagers who had gone on a killing rampage at Columbine High School [on April 20, 1999]. Columbine! That previous April, I shut off that news coverage even faster than I had tried to shut off CNN earlier on this day. I was more concerned with little girls in pigtails carrying their baby dolls than I was with teenagers in trench coats carrying semiautomatic weapons. Was this because I was insensitive? Or was it because today's horror happened to children so similar to my own? Whatever the reason, I felt ashamed. Ashamed that I had somehow convinced myself that this wasn't my problem. And I felt sick.

Now that I was focused on the issue, and I was online, I read about shootings I should have taken more interest in. Just that past Fourth of July weekend, I had somehow glazed right over the news of the shooting death of former Northwestern basketball coach Ricky Byrdsong. I had gone to graduate school at Northwestern. I wasn't much of a basketball fan, true, but now that I thought about it, the one and only time I did go to a collegiate basketball game was on March 30, 1981—the day President Reagan and his press secretary, James Brady, were shot. I certainly remembered that shooting, but other than making a mental note not to stand too close in public to my then-boss, Senator Long, I didn't think much about the facts of the shooting, except that I knew that it had to do with some nut trying to impress the actress Jodie Foster.

How Do Killers Get Guns?

Now, because of the JCC shooting, for the first time I was really curious to know just how these nuts manage to get their hands on guns at all.

In the case of Ricky Byrdsong, the shooter, Benjamin Nathaniel Smith—a member of a white supremacist hate group who had a history of violence and who was under a court restraining order secured by an ex-girlfriend—bought a gun through a classified newspaper ad and went on a Fourth of July killing spree in Illinois and Indiana. He targeted African-Americans, Jews, and Asians. In the end, he killed two people and wounded another nine. Smith shot people in Chicago, two of its suburbs, three other Illinois cities, and Bloomington, Indiana. In addition to Ricky Byrdsong—who was shot while walking with his children through their Skokie, Illinois, neighborhood—Smith killed Won-Joon Yoon, a South Korean doctoral student at Indiana University.

Gun Control Laws Hardly Exist

As I surfed the Web that night, I read about gun laws in this country, and I was shocked at how bad—or nonexistent they are. There are only six federal laws concerning gun control, and they have such giant loopholes that I could drive my minivan through them. Outside of these six very skeletal laws, there are a mishmash of roughly 300 state and local laws that have been cobbled together in an attempt to put a stop to this very real public health crisis.

The stronger state laws would work better if only they were uniform across the states. For example and hypothetically, a college student down South who needs to finance his spring break vacation can legally purchase guns in bulk in a state with poor laws, load them into his SUV, drive up I-95, and make a killing (literally) by selling them illegally to teenagers in New York City. Apparently, scenarios like this were playing out every day in this country.

One solution, offered by former presidential candidate Bill Bradley, was to make it illegal at the federal level to load up on all of these guns in the first place. But the gun lobby pooh-poohed that by saying that limiting gun purchases to only one a month would put an unnecessary burden on gun collectors. Well, let's weigh that for a moment, shall we? The burden of burying children versus the burden of having to wait a month to add a new gun to the gun rack. Which side did Congress pick? The kids? Or the collectors?

Gun Control Is a Taboo

It is hard to say, because bills like this never make it out of committee, much less to the floor for a roll-call vote. As I read on, it sounded like a lot of these congressmen must be getting drunk at gun-lobby parties, because their reasons for not pressing for these laws were so ludicrous. Thankfully, a few members of Congress did sound sober and were trying to change things. But not with a whole lot of success.

In fact, the Byrdsong shooting came on the heels of Congress utterly disrespecting the mothers and fathers of the dead kids at Columbine when it failed to close the lethal "gun-show loophole" when it had the chance—a loophole that enabled a private seller at a gun show to sell a gun legally without even being required to check a photo ID, much less run a background check on people who shouldn't own guns, such as kids like the 18-year-old girl who bought guns this way for the Columbine killers.

To be honest, I didn't even know then what a gun show was. The Violence Policy Center Web site described them as "Tupperware parties" for the criminally insane. That was enough to catch my attention. Certainly not everyone who attends a gun show is a Timothy McVeigh [an American terrorist responsible for the Oklahoma City bombing in 1995]. Even my dentist later told me he likes to go to them. But it sure sounded like any teenager or terrorist who couldn't buy a gun legally from a law-abiding licensed dealer could just go to a gun show and buy one from a private dealer who is not held to the same federal laws requiring background checks as is his licensed counterpart.

A Wake-up Call

Why was I so outraged now? Did I write to my congressman after Columbine and demand action? I did not. What, I wondered, would I do now?

When Buford Furrow surrendered to the FBI a day or two after Granada Hills, I, and the rest of the country, learned that he was a convicted felon with a history of mental illness. He should never have been in possession of a gun, but he walked right through a loophole, bought guns, and shot at children, all the while claiming that his actions were "a wake-up call to kill Jews." Well, he woke me up, although not quite as he had intended. I still wasn't sure—now that I was awake—what I was supposed to do. I have to admit, my first thought was to pull my kids out of the Jewish Community Center. I had enrolled Lili and Phoebe in a local JCC nursery school to help educate them in the faith of their father, half-brothers, and probably most important, my Jewish mother-in-law. But I wouldn't keep them there if it meant making them targets for mentally disturbed anti-Semitic gun nuts, like the Buford Furrows of the world. Maybe they should be raised instead as Southern Baptists, which is what my mother was, or as Catholics, like my father and me, especially since I had never heard of anyone shooting up a Baptist or Catholic Church—at least not then.

After August 10, 1999, I felt I needed to make some hard decisions in my life. But I wasn't sure at the time what those decisions would be, except that I would damn well stop reading the newspapers only for the gossip pages and start taking notice of the stories about gun violence. And there were plenty. The first to catch my attention was about the drive-by shooting death of an 11-year-old choirboy from Brooklyn. His name was Kelvin, and based on his picture, be was adorable. Apparently, he was also a wonderful kid who was beloved by many. The article quoted a police lieutenant named Eric Adams, who was a member of an organization called 100 Blacks in Law Enforcement. Lt. Adams was clearly shaken up by Kelvin's death, as he was by the many unnecessary gun deaths he had seen in his Brooklyn neighborhood. He used his chance to speak up in print to beg Americans to end their love affair with guns. Too many kids were getting killed, he said.

I decided on the spot that I wanted to meet Eric Adams, and so I called his office. Maybe he would he able to tell me, a formerly apathetic American citizen, what I could do to help. It would be days before Lt. Adams returned my call. In the interim, I became a voracious Web surfer, hungry to learn as much about the policy side of the gun issue as possible. I read about initiatives to childproof guns that were derailed by the gun lobby, probably for the same reasons that the automotive lobby tried to block the mandatory installation of airbags and seat belts. Taking safety measures at the manufacturing level costs money and may take pennies from profits, was the thinking of many lobbyists. Was saving lives worth so little, I wondered?

Gun Control Groups Inform the Public

I logged on so much to the Web site of Handgun Control Inc. (HCI) that if they rewarded me with frequent flier miles, I could have flown around the world at least a dozen times. Their Web site and those of the other national gun-control groups, like the Violence Policy Center, were extremely informative. But none showed me how to get directly involved in the issue beyond donating money or writing a letter to my congressman. I resolved to do both, but it just didn't seem like enough.

I called directory assistance in Washington, D.C., and asked for the phone numbers of the gun-control organizations. I specifically wanted to reach HCI because I knew that Sarah Brady, the wife of James Brady, President Reagan's wounded press secretary, was their chairwoman. She was the most well-known gun-control advocate in the country at that time. She was also a mom.

But the number for Handgun Control Inc. wasn't listed. I assumed (correctly) that this was probably a measure taken to prevent gun nuts from harassing the staff. I tried to contact a few other of the national gun control groups by phone but came up against the same roadblock. How hard would I have to work, I thought, to find an organization I could give my time to? . . .

First Steps Toward the Million Mom March

Someone once said that inspiration is really nothing more than all of life's experiences colliding at the same moment. And for me, this collision took place on the LIRR [Long Island Railroad]. Most people who have been inspired to take action rarely feel the need to explain how they got from point A to point B, but because so much disinformation has been spread about the creation of the Million Mom March, I feel the need to set the record straight. What I want to tell you is this: It wasn't because I had worked on Capitol Hill for a few years, or that I had worked in television or for *CBS News*, or because I was a publicist that I wanted to take action, though all of this experience would come in handy once the Million Mom March was a reality (especially being a publicist). The experience that had given me the organizational skills—and the courage—to decide to take a stand and get involved in gun control was simply this: my time as a mother.

So much gun violence surrounds us, and unless we're caught in the crossfire, most of us don't pay much attention to it. But if you stop to think about it, you'd be surprised to see where guns may have, however remotely, touched your own life. Only after I decided to get involved in gun control did it occur to me that a random pattern of gun violence runs through my own life. There was my father, terrified but resilient, staring down the barrel of a gun behind the counter of his pharmacy; there was Senator Russell Long, for whom I'd worked on Capitol Hill, who had lost his father to an assassin's bullet.

Despite all of these bullets whizzing by, it wasn't until a man named Buford Furrow urged other gun nuts like himself to target children just like mine that I decided that a mother's got to do what a mother's got to do.

Sitting on the train that day, with a wary mother and her two kids sitting across from me and a threatening-looking man toting a bag that carried something in it that looked suspiciously like an assault rifle, I took out a pen and an old manila envelope—the only paper in my bag—and started to write. And what I wrote was a simple one-page plan on how I might get myself and other moms to stand up, speak up, and make gun control a reality. Those few words on that torn manila envelope were the rough draft for what became known as the Million Mom March. How did I come up with this name? Just that day, in the *New York Post*, there was an article about a controversy on a permit dispute for the Million Youth March. Being a good publicist, I realized that this "Million March" brand had built-in news value. So I decided to borrow the name.

I then pulled my calendar out of my bag, shuffled through the pages, and picked a date: May 14, 2000. It was Mother's Day. That had a nice ring to it. I counted back from that date to today's date, and it was almost exactly 9 months. I couldn't believe it. It was the gestation period known and universally understood by all mothers! There is a god, I remember thinking, and she's not only a publicist, but she's also a mom!

The Fear of Being Shot

The train pulled into Penn Station. The scary, tattooed man stood up to disembark and unzipped his bag. The other mom and I held our breath. Out came an umbrella, its spokes all broken and tangled. "Guess I won't be needing this anytime soon," he said to no one in particular. He then stuffed it into a trash bin on the platform. Clearly this man was not the neo-Nazi maniac with an assault weapon I had imagined him to be. But what about next time? And, more important, why do we have to live in fear of a next time?

By the time I reached my midtown office that morning, I was no longer just a mother and part-time publicist. I was a woman on a mission. When I had a break in my work, I logged on to www.register.com, the company mentioned in the article I had read on the train, and I—a card-carrying technophobe—easily registered the new Web site: www.millionmommarch-.com.

I then called the Capitol Hill Police in Washington, D.C. (I knew the capitol switchboard number by heart from my stint with the senators back in the 1980s.) Officer Raymond, who answered, was very polite. He didn't even snicker when I asked for an application to march on Washington next Mother's Day, and he promptly faxed me a permit application. I filled out the details with as much information as I had, which, at this point, was very little. All I recall writing was that I was going to lead a rally of mothers in support of sensible gun laws. There was a line on the application for the estimated attendance for the event. Hmmm. I didn't know. Maybe 10,000, I wrote.

I faxed it back and waited 15 minutes. Then, impatiently, I called back.

"So, did you get it?" I said, my foot tapping on the floor.

"Yes, I got it," Officer Raymond replied, matter-of-factly.

"And?" I asked.

"And, we're passing this baby around like one hot potato." He sounded like he meant this.

"Why?" I asked.

"Because," he said, "we all know that our own mothers will be there."

At first I didn't understand what he meant. But I learned, soon after that conversation, that two Capitol Hill police officers had been shot and killed while on duty the year before. I realized that Officer Raymond was probably remembering this senseless crime and his fallen colleagues when he made that comment. Of course their mothers would be there. Maybe 10,000 wasn't such a pie-in-the-sky figure after all.

Next I called my husband, Jeff, at his office, to give him a heads-up. I tried to sound as nonchalant as I could. "Honey," I said. "I'm planning to organize a march on Washington." And then, almost as an afterthought, I asked him, "Is that okay with you?" I thought Jeff would laugh, but I guess he knew me better than I knew myself. He didn't seem to doubt for a moment that I was serious. But he was concerned. "Going against the gun lobby? That sounds kind of dangerous." And, with that, he fled to Peru. Okay. He didn't actually flee to Peru; he went there on a business trip. But in the 6 days he was gone, the Million Mom March completely overtook me, the kids, the house, the neighborhood—it was like the blob [referring to the 1950s horror movie], only pink (our official color), and it was oozing over everything. . . .

I knew our original mission statement by heart. It had been vetted by our original corps of sponsors, our mother-in-law focus groups, editorial writers (some of whom worked for conservative newspapers), and, of course, many moms. While this statement evolved and changed over the course of the next 9 months, I still love this first draft that Alison Hendrie wrote with such raw passion. I've added some corrections here, to show that, though we might not have had all of our facts straight when we wrote this, our hearts were in the right place.

ORIGINAL MISSION STATEMENT

September 1999

Million Mom March mother's day 2000 is dedicated to the mission of educating our children and our country about the life-threatening danger of guns.

Although simplistic and seemingly self-evident, this mission is in direct conflict with a powerful, heavily financed cultural and political juggernaut which justifies misuse of guns with references to freedom, liberty, and the American Dream.

We, the mothers, know that life is the first pursuit promised by our Constitution. *(My mother-in-law, a former teacher, had to point out that the Constitution doesn't guarantee life— that would be the Declaration of Independence. Oops.)* Our children's lives far outweigh the right for just anyone, especially juveniles, to carry a semiautomatic assault weapon or a Saturday Night Special.

While we acknowledge that guns may be necessary for hunting, law enforcement, and national security, the proliferation of firearms intended for one purpose only—killing another human being—has become untenable.

We believe that it is only common sense for individuals who want to exercise their Second Amendment rights to be required to submit to a sensible waiting period and background check before they are permitted to purchase a gun from any person or place. *(We had to change this after a supporter wrote to our Web site and very gently suggested that we read the Second Amendment. We did, and oops again: The Second Amendment doesn't actually guarantee individual rights. This would be corrected in the next edition.)*

We believe that every responsible and law-abiding gun owner should welcome legislation requiring safety locks on all handguns sold in the future. *(We had to add the words, "built-in safety locks" because as it was explained to us, a detachable trigger lock is more likely to end up in a junk drawer. We learned that the technology does exist to make built-in locks, and it works in much the same way as the childproof bottle caps created by aspirin manufacturers.)*

We call on all officers of the law to assume a no-nonsense approach in enforcing existing gun laws and to join us in our mutual crusade for stronger legislation.

We call on all child-friendly, nonviolent stores, companies, and corporations to sponsor us in these pursuits by advertising our message that guns—in the wrong hands—are simply unacceptable. In turn, we, the mothers, promise to patronize all child-friendly, nonviolent sponsors who join us in this mission.

We call on the like-minded to work with community law-enforcement agencies to offer swaps of meaningful goods and services for guns. We call on the proper authorities to then destroy the repossessed weapons.

Our aim is to recruit—from all walks of life—mothers, grandmothers, stepmothers, godmothers, foster mothers, future mothers, and all others willing to be "honorary mothers" in this crusade. Our goal is to educate and mobilize the mothers of America to this cause. Our commitment as voting citizens is to realize our goals by Mother's Day 2000.

A Mother Loses Her Son to Gun Violence

Karin Wilson

In the following viewpoint the author describes the pain of losing her only child, nineteen-year-old Christian, to gun violence. She details her decision to become proactive and fight gun violence through participating in the Million Mom March. Karin Wilson is a volunteer for the Brooklyn, New York, chapter of the Million Mom March.

I lost my beloved son, my only child Christian, on 3 Dec 1999. Just 28 days after he turned 19, he was a man-child, not quite an adult but past adolescence. The millennium came in a way I could have never imagined. The pain is indescribable; the magnitude of my loss makes me inconsolable. I've been wronged and robbed! I'm from the United States, I live in the state of New York, born and raised in the borough of Brooklyn. The US is one of the most powerful and technologically advanced countries on this planet. We haven't fought a war in this country since the American Civil War, a war that was fought from 1861–1865.

Yet in my neighbourhood and in many others in this country we hear gunshots at night. Parents start doing silent head-counts of their children after hearing the sound of gunshots. We have neighbours, friends and family members who were either maimed or killed with a firearm. Because of my son's death I became part of the largest grassroots anti-gun violence movement in the United States.

Part of the Future Is Gone

Let me tell you how my life has changed. I won't have the comfort of my son looking after me in my old age. I won't

Karin Wilson, "Trying to Make a Change," *Survivors: Women Affected by Gun Violence Speak Out*, August 20, 2007. Reproduced by permission.

have my son around making sure I'm eating well, taking my medications properly, taking care of my bills, making sure my house is warm in winter, and the sidewalks shovelled and de-iced when it snows. I don't have any more graduations to attend, or opportunities to applaud successful career achievements. I no longer hear funny stories or jokes (and I was told my son was one of the funniest guys around, he kept people laughing and feeling good). But worst of all I can't look at or touch him anymore.

You probably have wives and husbands, children and grandchildren. You know it's through our children we get a little bit of immortality. You know that your face, your body type, your values are going to be around long after you're gone . . . because of your children. Children are our legacy.

Well I was robbed, and it looks like I won't have a legacy now. My face, my body type, my values will probably disappear when I die—it doesn't look like any part of me will appear in the future. In the next century it will be as if I never, ever existed. And that's pretty sad.

I've learned that there is nothing like definite, overt action to overcome the inertia of grief. Most of us have someone who needs us. If we haven't, we can find someone! So instead of praying for the strength to survive, I prayed for strength to give away. Then I joined the Million Mom March. I went from being a victim of gun violence to a survivor of gun violence. And now I'm an advocate for survivors.

I'm thoroughly committed to saving other children. Though I couldn't save my own child's life, I'm going to do all I can to save yours.

Action Against Gun Violence

I know it is possible to reduce the number of deaths and injuries caused by gun violence. Our children have the right to grow up in environments free from the threat of gun violence. My son certainly had that right which he didn't get.

Our children want to grow old. All humans have the right to be safe from gun violence in their homes, neighbourhoods, schools and places of work and worship.

Gun violence is a public health crisis of global proportions that harms not only the physical, but the spiritual, social and economic health of our families and communities. The Million Mom March has a slogan which I subscribe to 100%: 'No child's life should end with a bang.'

I'm trying to understand why my child had to die by gunshot, but I don't understand. If I had one wish it would be that all governments would monitor the manufacturing and distribution of firearms and bullets with the same degree of care that they use to monitor the removal of nuclear waste from reactors.

We have an opportunity to change laws and create real accountability on these items. We have to stand up now and be counted on to do the right thing.

What It Feels Like to Get Shot

Wade Meredith

In this viewpoint, Jesse, a gun-assault survivor, describes the impact of the bullet that almost killed him. He details the different sensations and emotions, and talks about the lasting damage, physically and emotionally, the attack caused. Wade Meredith is the author of the blog Healthbolt.

My name is Jesse (online name Danny Bishop). I myself was shot—in the chest—on November 27th, 1994, at point-blank range ... I can tell you—not from watching it happen—but from actually experiencing it, exactly what it was like. First of all, there was the most incredible, shocking impact you could ever imagine—equivalent with having an M-80 (quarter stick of dynamite) go off in your shirt pocket—and I can tell you, I was sent reeling. It felt like I was thrown back [a] good 2-to-5 feet or more, as my legs gave out on me. There was simultaneously, a feeling like a bomb went off *inside* of my chest, and that of being jack-hammered through my chest wall—all of this, all at once. Then, everything seemed to go into slow motion, as undoubtedly, a large amount of adrenaline was released from my adrenal medulla, causing my central nervous system synapses to fire faster—like a high-speed camera, producing a slow motion effect. I was later told that the bullet (not surprisingly) ricocheted around in my chest like a pinball, first penetrating my entire chest mass, fracture and bounce off my left scapula, hurl back through my chest again, fracture a rib, and then bounce back through, trace a path around another rib (and puncture the pleural lining of my left lung), next flying straight into my spinal column, fracturing my T-9 and T-10 thoracic vertebrae, and transecting my spinal cord (I am now paraplegic). Feeling all

Wade Meredith, "What's It Feel Like to Get Shot with a Gun?" Healthbolt.net, April 17, 2007. Reproduced by permission of the author.

of this, all at once, was ... like being shot three times or more, not to mention that waves of paresthesia (tingling) echoed and surged throughout my body. My feeling in my legs was gone, just like that, at the same time I was flying backward—into a chair and a desk. Oddly, at that moment, I was hell-bent on protecting my head.

A Terrible Impact

Finally, lying on the ground in that room, only a good 30 seconds or so post-impact, I felt my left lung begin to squeeze, and my breaths were agonizingly painful and terribly short. Every breath was a knife turning in my lung. Then, I began to lose my vision—like white-out erasing my visual field as I began to go into hypo-volemic shock (low blood volume). I lost my ability to see temporarily, and could not tell what was going on around me. Then I passed out for what was probably thirty minutes. It was a darn miracle that I did not die, as a doctor later told me. The bullet almost 'curved' around my heart, within a centimeter or two of hitting it or a major blood vessel (it could have easily hit me right in the inferior, or even the superior, vena cava, near the heart muscle, in which case death would have followed in 1–2 minutes or even fewer, and unconsciousness in thirty seconds or less.

Agonizing Pain

As to the question: 'Does a person writhe in agony?'—No, I personally did not *writhe* in agony, like I had been lit on fire, but I was instantly thrown into the most excruciating, truly agonizing experience of pain I have ever known—and I have had chronic spinal pain ever since. ... The reason I was not *writhing* in agony is I was knocked into a state of indescribable shock, and was incapable of much, if any movement. However, after waking up thirty minutes or so after passing out, I managed to sit up, despite my paralysis, and I still remember—even though my pain had diminished somewhat at that point ... the feeling of warm blood pouring down my shirt, and adding to the pool of blood underneath me. ... I lay there for about four more hours before someone found me—I could barely whisper, much less yell. ...

A Slow Recovery

I was also beginning to hurt so badly again that no words can describe it. It was horrible. Hospitalization was no picnic either, let me tell you. ... I finally regained around 98% lung capacity, amazingly, and then one month after arriving at Santa Clara Valley Medical Center in the Bay Area, California, I began Spinal Cord Injury Rehabilitation. I had to learn to deal with having little control over my bowels, having to learn how to do a 'bowel program' with suppositories and the fact that I had no feeling in my groin—meaning no future physical sexual feelings. [I have] no ability to masturbate—and still have a huge sex drive ... how do you like that? What made it worse was, before I was shot, at age 16, I had never had sex, and never had a girlfriend, even though I can say honestly I am, and have long been, a very attractive man. And even though I have had half a dozen girlfriends now, ten years later, dating was no fun ... having to explain my limitations. In October of 2003 however, I had one of the happiest days of my life, when I married my wife, Jennifer. My dad was my best man. However, even being married, and having a willing sexual partner, I find myself doing almost all of the pleasing, and I suppose I will never know what it is like to be inside a woman—to actually *feel* it at all. ... Any of you out there who have had the experience, count yourselves as lucky. Unless there's sex in the Hereafter—I suppose I will never know what sex is like. You have no idea how angry that makes me, and how much pent up sexual frustration a guy has after a decade of no orgasmic release. Hey, that may sound shallow, but *try it some time*. It's funny, though. So many people, when finding out I was shot in the chest, ask the same question. "Did it ...

hurt?" Um, yeah, it was the most agonizing thing I ever experienced, and could ever imagine experiencing, and so I can definitely say, 'It wasn't like a massage.' But hey, I understand what fascination people have with pain and extreme injury. After all, before I was shot, watching action movies, I wondered what it was like.

Gun Violence on Campus

Candace Murphy

After three highly publicized shootings in one week, Candace Murphy, in the following article recalls two personal incidents of gun violence and questions the soundness of American policy toward gun ownership. If innocent schoolchildren and bystanders can be harmed so easily by anyone old enough to buy a gun, she concludes, it might be time for legal action to make life safer. Candace Murphy is a news writer in California.

The three school shootings that happened around the country in the fall of 2006 were horrible. Sad. Inexplicably violent.

First there was that drifter, a guy who lived in his car, who walked into a Colorado school, held some girls hostage, then shot one as she tried to escape before killing himself. Then there was the disturbed teen who gunned down his school principal in Wisconsin. And finally, there was that truck driver in Pennsylvania who was so despondent that he entered the Amish school near his home, lined up some girls, and took them out, execution style, before killing himself.

But even though the headlines like "Who Will Save Our Children?" and "Now It's Outsiders Shooting in Schools" are all written, even though President George [W.] Bush is shocked and has announced a summit at the White House to discuss school violence, and even though *People* magazine, as we speak, is undoubtedly slapping together some sort of "Shocking Week in Our Schools" issue, the sad truth is that none of this is new.

Candace Murphy, "After Shootings in U.S. Schools, Gun Violence Back in Spotlight," *Oakland Tribune*, October 7, 2006. © 2006 ANG Newspapers. Reproduced by permission.

Violence Is More than Statistics

Oh, I could spout statistics. I could get on a soap box and say something like how America's gun laws and gun culture were responsible for these killings. I could point out that the number of deaths in schools last week is just another tick on the giant murder counter in the sky that will eventually rise to the 30,000 or so gun deaths that occur every year. I could even quote the James Brady Campaign to Prevent Gun Violence, which found that American kids are more likely to die from firearms than kids from any other industrialized nation.

Actually, Brady's statistics are like a sick twist on the old *Sesame Street* "One of these things is not like the other" game but instead it's a case of "One of these countries is not like the other." We have Japan, where guns killed zero children in 1997, and then we have the United States, where guns killed 5,285 that same year.

Wow. Talk about how "One of these things just doesn't belong."

But really, I don't want to talk about statistical evidence. No matter how shocking they are, statistics will just go in one ear and out the other. Instead, let's talk anecdotal evidence. My own anecdotal evidence.

Guns on Campus Are Commonplace

Believe it or not, I, despite my sheltered youth spent growing up in suburban Anchorage, Alaska, despite my nuclear familial upbringing, have had not one encounter with guns on campus, but two.

The first was back in high school. I was a senior, and since my first period was slotted as Independent Study French V, I of course used the time to sleep in and saunter into school just before second period.

Well, one day I was doing my usual saunter down the hall toward my locker, a good 10 minutes to spare before second period English started, when a SWAT team rushed passed me.

I'm not kidding. All that was missing was the TV theme music. These guys had the charcoal black uniforms, the bullet-proof vests, helmets, goggles and scary looking weapons that were either automatic or semi-automatic, who knows, I didn't stop to ask, and when one of them yelled at me to go to my classroom I didn't ask why.

It didn't take long to find out what was happening, though. Minutes after I settled into a desk in my second period homeroom, the principal came on the loudspeaker. A big believer in sharing information—so much so that we called his weekly addresses over the loudspeaker "Fireside Chats"—the principal told us not to be worried, but that there was a hostage situation in the archery classroom.

Apparently, a guy who didn't attend our school, or any school, was upset that his girlfriend had dumped him, and was holding her and the rest of her archery class at bay with a gun. The principal assured us the situation would be taken care of quickly, since the SWAT team had arrived.

Unfortunately, though, the principal didn't realize that this particular Fireside Chat was being broadcast to not only all the students and teachers that were wondering what was going on, but to the archery room as well. Hearing the particulars of his breakup and of the SWAT team over the loudspeaker, the guy with the gun freaked out.

Thankfully, the situation somehow ended with no one killed. I'm not sure how, because everyone who wasn't in the archery room got to leave school not too long after the Fireside Fiasco, and I went to the Olive Garden for some hard-earned bread sticks and salad. But I know no one was seriously injured.

That wasn't the case with the other gun incident I witnessed. That one happened when I was a senior in college, and for that one, I was way too close to the action.

Because even anecdotal evidence gets wearisome, I'll be brief: There were two groups of kids, one might call them gangs, that were angry at each other. One of the kids pulled out a gun, shot it, and the next thing I knew the woman 10 feet away from me and standing at the bus stop had crumpled to the ground, blood bubbling out of a hole in her boot.

Sorry, but I have a problem with these "guns don't kill people, people kill people" zealots. All that woman wanted was the bus, not a bullet in her foot. Look—the right to keep and bear arms meant a whole different thing back when the Constitution was written, but maybe some people won't realize that until they're at the wrong end of the barrel and the vagaries of the Second Amendment have escaped them.

Anyway, it would have been best if neither of these incidents had happened. And at the time, there was a hubbub in the papers and among the local politicians, all grumbling how guns were dangerous and how something must be done.

Has anything? Not really. Gun violence happens disturbingly frequently in our schools and outside of them year after year. Because the latest spate of shootings has made for a grisly threesome—an unholy trinity of deadly incidents in the span of a week or so—gun violence will make the rounds on the talk shows, in the papers, in columns like this one.

But when do we stop talking and start doing?

CONTEMPORARY
ISSUES
COMPANION

CHAPTER 4

Deterring Gun Violence

Gun Control Laws Do Not Prevent Crime

National Rifle Association

Gun control laws, the authors of the following viewpoint claim, do not help keep Americans safe from gun violence. Instead of curtailing the right to bear firearms, the authors suggest that current laws be enforced and that violent criminals be punished without probation. Established in 1871 as a gun and shooting sports promotional organization, the National Rifle Association [NRA] is today also the largest, most powerful lobby for gun owners' rights through its Institute for Legislative Action.

So overwhelming is the evidence against the myth that "gun control" prevents crime, that it borders on the absurd for anti-gun groups to try to perpetuate it.

Violent crime peaked in the United States in 1991, and since that time gun prohibition and gun control laws have been eliminated or made less restrictive at the federal, state and local levels. Examples include:

- Twenty-five states have eliminated prohibitive or restrictive carry laws, in favor of Right-to-Carry (RTC) laws; there are 40 RTC states today.

- The federal Brady Act's waiting period on handgun sales expired in 1998, in favor of the NRA-supported National Instant Criminal Background Check, and some states concurrently or thereafter eliminated waiting periods or purchase permit requirements.

National Rifle Association, "Fables," nraila.org, May 24, 2006. Reproduced by permission.

- The federal "assault weapon" ban expired in 2004.

- Forty-seven states now prohibit local jurisdictions from imposing gun laws more restrictive than state law.

- Congress and 33 states have prohibited frivolous lawsuits against the firearm industry.

- Congress has prohibited the release of firearm tracing data, except to law enforcement agencies for purposes of bona fide criminal investigations in which they are involved.

- All states now have hunter protection laws, 46 have range protection laws, and 44 protect the right to arms in their constitutions.

Partly as a result of the relaxation of gun controls, the number of privately-owned guns has risen by about 75 million since 1991, to an all-time high of approximately 250 million guns in the United States.

Anti-gun groups regularly claim that eliminating gun controls and increasing gun ownership necessarily leads to severe increases in violent crime. But from 1991–2006 (the most recent year of data available) violent crime dropped 38%. Among the four categories of violent crime, murder dropped 42%, rape 27%, robbery 45%, and aggravated assault 34%. Preliminary figures released by the FBI indicate that violent crime dropped again in 2007. The Justice Department refers to current rates as a "historic low."

Studies conducted for Congress by independent researchers under the auspices of the National Institutes of Justice, the Congressional Research Service, and the Library of Congress, and other studies conducted by the National Academy of the Sciences, the Centers for Disease Control and Prevention, and independent researchers (including some who support gun control on philosophical grounds) have found no evidence that gun control reduces crime in this country or overseas.[1]

Some of the more obvious examples of gun control's failure to reduce crime (based, unless otherwise noted, on data from the FBI's Uniform Crime Reports) include:

- Washington, D.C.'s ban on handgun sales took effect in 1977 and by the 1990s the city's murder rate had tripled. During the years following the ban, most murders—and all firearm murders—in the city were committed with handguns. (Metropolitan Police Dept. of D.C.)

- Chicago imposed handgun registration in 1968, and murders with handguns continued to rise. Its registration system in place, Chicago imposed a D.C.-style handgun ban in 1982, and over the next decade the annual number of handgun-related murders doubled. (Chicago Homicide Dataset.)

- California increased its waiting period on retail and private sales of handguns from five to 15 days in 1975 (reduced to 10 days in 1996), outlawed "assault weapons" in 1989, subjected rifles and shotguns to the waiting period in 1990, and increased the number of gun

1. Federal "assault weapon" ban: Roth, Koper et al., Impact Evaluation of the Public Safety and Recreational Firearms Use Protection Act of 1994, March 13, 1997, www.urban.org/url.cfm?ID=406797; Reedy and Koper, "Impact of handgun types on gun assault outcomes: a comparison of gun assaults involving semiautomatic pistols and revolvers," *Injury Prevention* 2003, http://ip.bmjjournals.com/cgi/reprint/9/2/151; Koper et al., "Report to the National Institute of Justice, an Updated Assessment of the Federal Assault Weapons Ban: Impacts on Gun Markets and Gun Violence, 1994–2003," June 2004, www.sas.upenn.edu/jerrylee/jlc-new/Research/Koper_aw_final.pdf; Wm. J. Krouse, Congressional Research Service Report for Congress, "Semiautomatic Assault Weapons Ban," Dec. 16, 2004. "Gun control," generally: Library of Congress, Report for Congress: "Firearms Regulations in Various Foreign Countries," May 1998, LL98-3, 97-2010; Task Force on Community Preventive Service, "First Reports Evaluating the Effectiveness of Strategies for Preventing Violence: Firearms Laws," *Morbidity and Mortality Weekly Report*, Oct. 3, 2003, www.cdc.gov/mmwr/preview/mmwrhtml/rr5214a2.htm; National Research Council, *Firearms and Violence: A Critical Review*, National Academies Press, 2005, http://books.nap.edu/books/0309091241/html/index.html.

banned as "assault weapons" in 2000. Yet since 1975, the state's annual murder rate has averaged 32% higher than the rate for the rest of the country.

- Maryland has imposed a waiting period and a gun purchase limit, banned several small handguns, restricted "assault weapons," and regulated private transfers of firearms even between family members and friends, yet for the last decade its murder rate has averaged 60% higher than the national rate, and its robbery rate has averaged highest among the states.

- New York has had a handgun licensing law since 1911, yet until the New York City Police Department began a massive crackdown on crime in the mid-1990s, the city's violent crime rate was among the highest of major U.S. cities.

- The federal Gun Control Act of 1968 imposed unprecedented restrictions relating to firearms nationwide. Yet compared to the five years before the law, the national murder rate averaged 50% higher during the five years after the law, 75% higher during the next five years, and 81% higher during the five years after that.

- States in which the Brady Act's waiting period was imposed between 1994–1998 had worse violent crime trends than other states.

Stricter Gun Control Might Have Prevented the Virginia Tech Massacre

The Economist

This viewpoint looks critically at the Virginia Tech massacre and finds that gun control laws, and their enforcement, might have prevented the mentally disturbed killer from obtaining guns and shooting his peers and professors.

"You caused me to do this." That was Cho Seung-hui's excuse for murdering 32 people. Police found an essay in the young student's room that appeared to blame everyone but himself for what he was about to do. In it, he raged against religion, women, rich kids, debauchery and the "deceitful charlatans" at Virginia Tech, where he was studying English.

It was the worst peacetime shooting in American history. Investigators are still scrambling to work out what happened when, but a combination of announcements, leaks and witnesses suggest that it went something like this. Around 7.15 in the morning on April 16th, [2007,] in a dormitory called West Ambler-Johnston Hall, Cho shot and killed Emily Hilscher, an attractive 19-year-old would-be vet. Around the same time, he shot Ryan Clark, a popular member of the university marching band. Why he chose these two as his first victims is unknown. Rumours that he was attracted to Miss Hilscher are, inevitably, circulating. Mr Clark may have been shot because he tried to intervene.

On finding the bodies, the police assumed it was a domestic dispute and sought Miss Hilscher's boyfriend, who had

The Economist, "The Virginia Tech Massacre: In the University of Death," Economist-.com, April 19, 2007. Copyright © The Economist Newspaper Limited 2007. Republished with permission of *The Economist,* conveyed through Copyright Clearance Center, Inc.

dropped her off at the dormitory that morning in his pick-up truck. They found him, pulled him over and questioned him.

Meanwhile, Cho was mailing a manifesto to NBC News. It included pictures of him posing with guns, video clips and a rambling and obscene diatribe against wealthy people. At 9:05, while police were still pre-occupied with Miss Hilscher's boy-friend, Cho entered Norris Hall, a block of classrooms half a mile from Ambler-Johnston. He locked the doors with chains to stop people escaping. Then he walked into classrooms, one by one, and tried to kill everyone inside. He had two guns: a Glock 9mm and a Walther P22. Both are semi-automatic: they fire bullets as quickly as you can keep pulling the trigger. Each Glock magazine held 15 rounds; the Walther's held 10.

He Killed Silently

Survivors said the gunman killed without saying a word. He shot teachers and students at close range, in the face, in the mouth, anywhere. He put about three bullets into each victim, to make sure. Every time he emptied a magazine, he reloaded with skill and speed. He had plenty of ammunition. He kept on killing until police burst into Norris Hall. Then he shot himself. His face was so badly disfigured that police found it hard, at first, to identify him.

Some of his classmates had a hunch, though. When the news broke that a gunman was shooting people at random, several guessed it was Cho. He had always been quiet in class—in fact, he rarely spoke to anyone. He hid behind sun-glasses, a hat and a blank expression. But his classmates found him intimidating. It was his imagination that alarmed them.

He wrote two short plays for a creative-writing class. Nearly every line speaks of gore. The cardboard dialogue sug-gests an author who never really listened to other people. And the plots are suffused with anxious fury: about money, sex, re-ligion and overbearing adults.

Student Was Very Disturbed

In one play, called "Richard McBeef", a 13-year-old boy sits in his bedroom throwing darts at his stepfather's picture, muttering: "You don't think I can kill you, Dick? You don't think I can kill you? Gotcha. Got one eye. Got the other eye." The 13-year-old protagonist thinks his stepfather is a paedophile and a murderer, and that he has covered up his conspiracies. The play ends with the stepfather killing the boy.

In 2005 two female students complained to the police that Cho was stalking them, but declined to press charges. Police warned him off but did not arrest him because he had made no specific threats. A district court found reason to believe him "mentally ill" and "an imminent danger to self or others" and ordered him to undergo a psychiatric test. But the examination found "his insight and judgment are normal" and he was discharged.

He bought a gun on February 9th, at a pawnshop, and another on March 16th, at a gun shop in a nearby town. Both sales were legal. Cho was a native South Korean, but he had lived in America since he was eight years old. His family owned a dry-cleaning business in northern Virginia. Cho was a legal, permanent resident. He showed the gun dealer three forms of identification: a Virginia driving licence, a cheque book with a matching address and an immigration card.

The Gun Sale Was Legal

A quick background check showed he had no criminal record, so he was entitled, under Virginia law, to buy one gun each month. The gunshop owner insisted he found nothing suspicious about the clean-cut college boy.

Cho's victims—and he injured as many as he killed—were a fair cross-section of Virginia Tech. There were teachers and students, engineers and international-studies majors. One professor, Liviu Librescu, a 76-year-old Holocaust survivor, blocked the door of his classroom with his body to slow Cho's entrance. This bought enough time for his students to jump out of the window. But not enough for Mr Librescu himself to escape.

Many people asked how the horror might have been averted. Some complained that Virginia Tech should have warned students immediately after the first shootings, rather than waiting two hours, that the campus should have been "locked down" straight away, and that security at universities in general is too lax.

With hindsight, it is clear that early warnings might have been useful. But police did not know who they were looking for or what kind of threat he posed until it was too late. Locking down the entire campus is tricky when the campus is the size of a small town. And American universities in general are extremely safe places. So guarding student dormitories is hardly the most urgent task for the police. Most Virginia Tech students seem to think that the university coped just about as well as it could have.

The Lessons to Be Learned

Some critics wondered why more could not have been done about Cho's obviously troubled mental state. The question is, what? Until [that] week he had harmed no one, so it is not clear that there was enough justification for medicating him against his will or locking him up. Probably the most fruitful lessons to be learned from Virginia Tech concern guns.

The day after the shooting, the flags were flying at half-mast outside the Virginia headquarters of the National Rifle Association (NRA). America's mighty gun lobby tries to keep a respectfully low profile at times like these. But it responds to the challenges that inevitably arise when the weapons it champions are used to kill innocents.

Some Democrats called for tighter gun controls. Senator Dianne Feinstein of California lamented that "shootings like these are enabled by the unparalleled ease with which people procure weapons in this country" and said she hoped that the tragedy would "reignite the dormant effort to pass common-sense gun regulations". But most politicians showed little enthusiasm for this idea, President George [W.] Bush said that "now is not the time to do the debate [on gun control]". Harry Reid, the Senate's Democratic majority leader, warned against a "rush to judgment"....

Why Politicians Buckle

The academic debate about whether guns save more innocent lives than they cut short, or vice versa, may never end. Most Americans are inclined to believe the latter. But politicians bow to the gun enthusiasts because their beliefs are much more likely to determine how they vote.

In the 1990s, the Democrats tried to impose modest gun controls. For example, in 1994 President Bill Clinton signed a ban on assault weapons—military-type rapid-fire rifles with no conceivable civilian use except perhaps to defend one's home against a whole gang of drug-dealers. President Bush allowed this ban to lapse in 2004, however, and the Democrats are convinced that gun control helped them lose elections in 1994 and 2000.

The reason is that, no matter how often the Democrats promise not to take away hunters' rifles, the NRA treats any curb on gun rights as a first step towards complete disarmament. And without their 240m [million] guns, it argues, Americans will be defenceless not only against criminals but also against tyranny. The NRA draws on history to support its arguments. The first European settlers conquered America with guns; British soldiers tried to confiscate them, but the Americans revolted and shot off the superpower's yoke.

Gun Control Loses Elections

This may be a selective view of history, but it is still relevant, for two reasons. One is that the notion of a right to bear arms is enshrined in the Constitution. The other is that the NRA constantly exaggerates threats to gun-owners. Its sells books such as "Thank God I Had a Gun: True Accounts of Self-Defence". It relentlessly publicises the fact that police in New Orleans, during the looting spree that followed Hurricane Katrina, confiscated some legally-held guns. And its chief, Wayne LaPierre, has peddled for years the absurd theory that the United Nations is plotting to take away Americans' guns.

Few urban Americans swallow this twaddle, which is why many cities have stiff anti-gun laws. But some rural people do, and plenty more love hunting and think anti-gun Democrats are wusses. To counter this image and court rural votes, the Democratic Party has largely abandoned its gun-control crusade. Its presidential candidates now play up their love of hunting, real or otherwise. In several states, the party has recruited serious gun enthusiasts as candidates. The Democratic governor of Montana boasts that he has more guns than he needs, but not as many as he would like. And the Democrats won control of the Senate [in 2006] by fielding a pro-gun war hero to snatch a pro-gun state from a pro-gun Republican incumbent. That state was Virginia.

Banning Guns Is Not Enough to Stop Campus Violence

Chris McGoey

In this viewpoint, the author asserts that banning all guns is not the solution to gun violence, since America is already saturated with firearms. Instead teachers and parents have to intervene when a student shows signs of violent behavior. In a society where violent video games and violence in the media are flooding homes, parents and teachers have to make sure that they address the problem and teach alternatives to violent aggression. Chris McGoey is an author, trainer, and speaker and maintains the Web site Crime Doctor.

Guns, children, and school should never be used in the same sentence. But over the last few years a trend has emerged causing the media to report incidents of gun violence in our schools. This has got to stop! The question is how do we stop it?

A knee-jerk response like "ban all the guns" is an oversimplification of a more complex problem. It has been reported that in the United States guns are manufactured at a rate of about 18,000 per day and have an estimated life of about 400 years each. It should be no surprise then, to learn that in the United States there are more guns than there are adults. To think or believe that guns can be removed from every home in America is illogical, especially since our Constitution specifically guarantees our right to bear arms. In all fairness, however, the writers of our Constitution, over 200 years ago, were probably thinking about citizens having a slow-loading, single-shot Musket for civil defense against invaders. They could not possibly foresee the use of assault weapons at school and mass murder.

Chris McGoey, "Campus Security: Gun Violence at School," Crime Doctor, August 28, 2007. www.crimedoctor.com. Reproduced by permission of the author.

Another common solution offered is to control the public and private sale of guns. These regulations would further limit private sales to minors, prohibit sales of certain automatic weapons, and cause more registration of guns. All these methods may have some impact on the availability of guns in the future and will undoubtedly help the police locate more gun owners. Unfortunately, more laws and regulations tend to open up the black-market where gun transactions will continue to flourish illegally. All we have to do is look at our existing drug laws and our failed attempt at liquor prohibition to see that legislation is a slow process and has definite limitations.

Declining Crime Rate

Although gun violence is in the spotlight because of the recent pattern of school shootings, the violent crime rate and criminal incidents involving guns has been declining over the past several years. Arguably, gun violence should be increasing almost exponentially based on the number of guns in existence and the number of new guns being manufactured year after year.

The question of how to stop gun violence on campus may best be understood by looking at the connection between "where" the incidents occur, "who" is committing them, "who" are the intended victims, and "why." The most common thread is the location ... our high schools and middle schools. The second pattern that has emerged is that the perpetrators are also students. The third pattern is that the shooters were male and to varying degrees not a part of the mainstream school social structure.

Copycat Crimes

Why this level of violence continues to occur at schools, as opposed to some other place, is obvious. The first school shooting created media frenzy and the offending students became infamous. The massive media blitz creates a sick notoriety for those who want to make a statement by the massacre of fellow students. Clearly, a "copycat" game is now in play. Unfortunately, others may decide that they want to beat the record and get a higher body count. Aside from the media, it seems that the Internet is playing a role in spreading the word about violence, hate, and guns. For the first time in our history, anyone on the Internet can learn how to make a bomb or communicate anonymously with hate groups, or with terrorists.

I predict this sick copycat trend will pass and the period will be recorded as a dark time in our history. What is needed now is increased awareness, both at home and at school. Parents, teachers, and students need to communicate about the underlying issues and everyone needs to pay attention for the telltale signs of violence. Evidence of the potential for violence is often found in a student's home, on their computer, in their notebooks or in their locker at school.

Are Video Games to Blame?

Violent video games, like the first-person-shooters, may have influenced the mindless and surreal concept of randomly shooting students. At no other time in history could a young person have sat for hours in front of a video monitor and simulated the massacre of hundreds of people (or aliens) using a high-powered arsenal of weapons. This form [of] "electronic entertainment" does not represent reality because there are no consequences after pulling the trigger. Graphic shooter video games teach the player to seek out and destroy everything in their path while displaying the blood and guts in vivid color, 3-D, and with stereo sound effects. It is not surprising that a few of these video shut-ins may begin to fantasize about shooting other students they believe have tormented or shunned them while at school.

How to Stop Guns on Campus

Sure, we can make it more difficult to bring guns onto campus. But this will come at a cost of personal freedom. We can build a fortress-like school with higher fences, lock more doors, close the campus, install magnetometers and x-ray machines, and conduct pat downs and random locker searches. The problem is that the student violence could simply move to another public gathering place like a movie theater, a shopping mall, or a restaurant.

When someone is carrying a gun at school, usually other students will know, but won't say anything . . . that needs to change. Many times parents will observe a negative change in behavior of their children, but won't inquire or investigate the suspicious activity . . . that needs to change. Many parents allow their children to surf the web everyday, without knowing how to supervise their activity . . . this may be our greatest challenge. Teachers are our messengers and have the forum to promote discussions about the social and moral impact of hate, violence, guns, and computer video games . . . that subject needs to be incorporated into the mainstream curricula.

For now, our students need more social awareness, parental interaction, and protection by our existing laws. For the long term, our society needs to figure out how to deal with the availability of guns, how to handle the programming content on the Internet, in violent video games, and in movies. Children are our future and we need to help them find a balance between the rapidly changing technology and traditional social values.

Choice and Individual Responsibility Are More Effective than Laws in Reducing Gun Violence

J. Thomas Bennett

In the following viewpoint, the author writes that the debates over gun control are distracting from the real issues underlying gun violence. Neither gun lobbyists nor gun control campaigners seem to acknowledge that our culture is in need of reform, toward a reawakened sense of personal responsibility for one's own actions. J. Thomas Bennett is a frequent contributor to the Midway Review, *a journal of political and cultural thought.*

The current debate over gun control and media violence is misguided at best and harmfully misleading at worst. There are multiple causes for violence, and they are difficult to measure, predict or prevent. Looking at the issue honestly will involve tough questions about the nature of modern freedoms, our culture, and the sources of morality. In terms of current events and historical trends, there is a problem with violence in America. That much is clear, but the causes and solutions are not clear at all. In the earnest search for someone or something to blame for the [2007] Virginia Tech shootings, we need to start with a fresh view of where we are as a society.

Over the last two years [2005–2007], rates of violent crime have begun to rise nationwide, reversing the healthy, downward trend of the last decade. The current rise in violent crime is especially troubling considering the trend in decreasing violent crime rates that began in 1992 and lasted until late

J. Thomas Bennett, "After Virginia Tech: Gun Control, Culture, and Violence Today," *The Midway Review*, Spring 2007. Copyright © 2007 by The Midway Review. Reproduced by permission of the author.

2005. In the *New York Times*'s reporting on the issue [in 2007], blame is evenly spread for this reemerging social problem. "Local police departments blame several factors," the article said, including "easy access to guns and a willingness, even an eagerness, to settle disputes with them, particularly among young people." Roughly speaking, there are two issues here: access to guns and morality. Our solutions to the kind of violence we saw last week [at Virginia Tech], however, should not boil down to the false choice between liberal and conservative, gun control and morality.

Causes of Gun Violence

After the shootings at Virginia Tech, gun control has again become a hot topic, along with media violence and the general decay of our culture. Can anything new or helpful be said about these issues? They seem to be timeless controversies, with no definite answers except for those offered by the dogmatic. Everyone has easy answers, but what is needed is hard thought. Gun control, of course, was the instant response for some, but the idea that additional gun control laws would have averted the shooting is not logically or empirically valid.

The Gun Control Act of 1968 has prohibited the "mentally defective" from the purchase or possession of guns since its enactment. Mentally defective here includes being a danger to one's self or others, as determined by an official body. Cho [the shooter] should have been affected by this regulation. After checking in to a mental health institution, a Virginia magistrate found him a threat to himself. This finding was sufficient under the federal law to keep Cho from buying guns. A mistake occurred when mental health experts and the Virginia magistrate didn't execute the regulation by putting Cho in the database for background checks. The prevention of violence, in this case, could have been achieved through enforcing existing legislation. In one sense, the shooting was "caused" by a loophole. Yet, this leaves open the whole realm of motivations, and the separate means—aside from legally purchasing guns—that "caused" this violence. What of the willingness to use guns, cited by police officials as one cause of the nationwide increase in violent crime? The motivation for gun violence and violence overall is incredibly broad, at once personal and societal, dealing with basic issues of responsibility and values.

A Change in Culture Affects Gun Violence

Criminologist David Garland, who is no conservative, writes that the reasons for increased crime rates from the '60s to early '90s include "a reduction in the efficacy of social and self controls as a consequence of shifts in social ecology and changing cultural norms." This included "demands for instant gratification" and "the spread of a more 'permissive,' 'expressive' style of child-rearing." These ideas make true believers on the left uncomfortable. As an explanation for crime, culture seems to concede too much to conservatism. But if we're honest with ourselves, we have to admit that the last 40 years of social science and American experience haven't exactly refuted concerns about cultural changes. Social scientists have noted that violence and crime are actively encouraged and valued within some groups. I believe that we are facing a historically unprecedented pro-violence subculture. (We should note that the Tech shootings and school shootings around the world serve to de-racialize this insight.) The implications of this cultural change for criminal behavior are vast, but they haven't been fully explored. The bottom line is that informal social controls—non-legal, non-political constraints on behavior—have been weakened. Events like the Virginia shooting show that the influence of weakened informal social controls is growing. Younger people are becoming more violent, and this tendency is strongly reinforced by culture, not objective circumstances of abuse or deprivation. The Tech shootings could have as much to do with norms as with legislation.

I believe that criminal behavior today is connected to self-sustaining subcultures independent of what we would usually call a societal "cause," such as poverty or bullying. It would be absurd to claim that Cho felt a justified subjective sense of victimization, and that this explains his actions. The problem with Cho was that he had guns, and also that he had an immoral set of attitudes about violence, himself, and others. The solution to this problem is not "structural" or legislative. The solution is difficult to define, but it should primarily involve restoring the foundation of norms and trust that supported a safer society in the past. I think this is a legitimate idea that deserves to be taken seriously by academics and policymakers.

Responsibility on the Decline

Not to blame a single person, but after Freud, will, choice, and responsibility have been undermined. In 1950, psychologist Otto Rank wrote that "the essential problem of psychology is our abolition of the fact of will." The notion that no one is truly responsible for their actions has made its way into ideologies and our public thinking about violence. This essentially authorizes antisocial and violent behavior. [Stanton] Samenow [a psychologist and writer] and [Samuel] Yochelson [a psychiatrist who, with Samenow, writes about criminal behavior] wrote that the criminal often "blames forces outside himself for his crime or for making him the way he is. . . . This position is usually reinforced by current concepts and practices and often by the judicial attitudes and decisions of those who deal with criminals." It has become too easy to justify or rationalize almost any form of behavior, no matter how cruel. This is to be expected without a counterbalancing insistence on responsibility and decency.

Cho Seung-Hui blamed others for his actions. He was insulted to some degree—and responded with horrible violence—but being bullied or alienated did not cause him to do what he did. Again, what needs to be explained is the willingness on the part of young people—almost entirely male—to use forms of violence that were once out of the question. This seems to be a matter of societal norms, childrearing, and culture, not of abuse or legislation. Speaking into his camera, Cho said, "You had a hundred billion chances and ways to have avoided today. But you decided to spill my blood. You forced me into a corner and gave me only one option. The decision was yours. Now you have blood on your hands that will never wash off." This is a concise statement using cruelty and irresponsibility to justify violence in response to minor aggravation. Cho's statement expressed a false or exaggerated sense of grievance, reflecting a new and troubling attitude. According to psychologist Adrian Furnham, "We may have socialised young people . . . [to] find it easier and acceptable to blame their woes on others and society rather than on their own lack of ability and effort." Understanding, preventing, and even punishing that attitude is the real solution for such violence, if there is going to be one. That will entail a serious discussion of self control, modern freedoms, our culture, parental controls, and norms and their roots—including religion. Of course, this prescription gives credence to the supposedly conservative argument that values matter most. It is supposed to be a sign of enlightenment to snicker at "values." However, it wasn't progress for us to move as a society from overemphasizing values to completely neglecting them. If this seems like moralizing, it is—and that is not a problem. It is painfully obvious during times like these that a morality deficit is causing more problems than a morality excess. Withholding judgment and failing to take firm measures causes as much pain as being judgmental or harsh. The most powerful example of this is the way Cho was handled by educational, medical, and legal institutions. Virginia law could have prevented Cho's buying guns, if all involved had taken a more punitive or public safety–minded approach.

Society Ignores Warning Signs

Virginia law forbids you from having a gun if you're a stalker or have been involuntarily committed to an institution. In 2005, two female students reported being stalked by Cho, but didn't press charges. If they would have, and Cho had been convicted, he would have been ineligible to purchase firearms once a background check was done. There was another opportunity: campus police recommended Cho be detained for mental evaluation. He was evaluated, a doctor found him depressed, then a state magistrate found him a danger to himself due to mental illness, but not a threat to others. The magistrate recommended outpatient treatment instead of involuntary commitment. In hindsight, Cho should have been involuntarily committed, making him ineligible under Virginia law to purchase a firearm. Then the federal-state disconnect would not have been decisive. As it happened, "causation" for the shooting is spread out across civil society, university, government, and mental health bureaucracies—there was no simple, single "cause" in the usual sense of the term.

As with most issues in politics, we're given a false choice in the debate over the shootings: you can be liberal and say we need more gun control, and that the war in Iraq is proof of our nation's dark heart, or you can be conservative and say that we need more morals. This is not a real choice, it's a phony debate. The most relevant facts about the Virginia Tech killings will force us outside of the ideological box. If liberals are willing to admit that strong moral judgments could have altered Cho's choice of means, and if conservatives are willing to admit that gun control laws could have repressed Cho's motives, then we will have learned something from this inexcusable criminal act.

National Programs Are Needed to Deter Youth Violence

Kathleen Reich, Patti Culross, and Richard Behrman

This viewpoint focuses on the everyday dangers arising from gun ownership. Parents who bring guns into a household need to be educated about their safe use and storage, to keep their children out of harm's way. But not only parents have to be proactive in the fight against gun violence. Communities and law enforcement have to step up to prevent more lethal incidents. Kathleen Reich is a program officer in the Children, Families, and Communities Program of the Packard Foundation. Patti Culross is the director of the Department of Public Health, Injury and Violence Prevention Program in Los Angeles. Richard Behrman, editor in chief (1989–2004) of the Future of Children, *is senior vice president for Medical Affairs at the Lucile Packard Foundation for Children's Health in Palo Alto, California.*

No single policy solution will end youth gun violence in the United States; a wide repertoire of approaches is needed to address different aspects of the problem. Key strategies that may reduce youth gun violence include: reducing unsupervised exposure to guns among children and youth; strengthening social norms against violence in communities; enforcing laws against youth gun carrying; altering the design of guns to make them less likely to be used by children and youth; and, perhaps most importantly, implementing new legal and regulatory interventions that make it more difficult for youth to obtain guns. Parents, community leaders, policymakers, and researchers all have vital roles to play in implementing these strategies.

Kathleen Reich, Patti Culross, and Richard Behrman, "Children, Youth, and Gun Violence: Analysis and Recommendations," *The Future of Children*, August 25, 2007. Reproduced by permission.

Reducing Unsupervised Exposure to Guns

By monitoring their children's behavior, environments, and media use, parents can be the first line of defense in protecting children from gun violence. Parents who choose to keep guns in the home have a special responsibility to make sure that their children, and other children who visit their homes, do not have access to these weapons without supervision. Because research indicates that educational efforts aimed at persuading children and youth to stay away from guns or behave responsibly around them are of limited effectiveness, policymakers and public health experts need to find creative, effective ways to educate parents about the importance of keeping their children safe through parental monitoring and safe gun storage.

Parental Monitoring

Close parental supervision can help keep children away from dangerous environments and situations. Ethnographic research indicates that this approach may be especially effective in neighborhoods where violence is commonplace. Parents who monitor their children closely also may be able to spot signs of violent behavior in their children more easily.

In addition, parents should monitor their children's media use, including their use of computers and video games. The American Academy of Pediatrics recommends that parents watch programming with their children; limit screen time for all media, including computers and video games, to a total of one to two hours per day; use the V-chip to restrict viewing of violent television; avoid violent video games; and keep children's bedrooms media-free.

Safe Storage

As the American Academy of Pediatrics observes, the best way to prevent firearm injuries among children in the home is to remove guns from the home. However, some parents who use guns for sport or self-defense are unwilling to take this step. In recent years, some gun control advocates and firearms manufacturers have promoted an alternative: safe storage of guns in homes with children or where children are likely to visit. They have counseled parents who own guns to store them locked, unloaded, and separate from their ammunition.

Safe gun storage practices have the potential to decrease unintentional shootings by making guns less accessible to children and youth. Safe storage also may reduce criminal gun use by youth by decreasing their access to guns in the home and by deterring theft, which is a prominent supply source for the illegal market, where many youth obtain guns.

Guns in the Home Are Dangerous

Although some oppose safe storage because they believe it makes guns less accessible for self-defense, this concern must be weighed carefully against the risk that a child could find and use guns that are not stored safely. A 1999 study of young people under age 20 who were killed or injured in unintentional shootings in King County, Washington, found that 69% of these shootings took place in the young person's home, or in the residence of a relative or friend. As [researcher Tom W.] Smith . . . notes, more than 70% of Americans support enacting laws that require guns to be stored locked and/or unloaded. . . .

The Need for Parent Education

Although efforts to promote safe gun storage have been widespread in recent years, studies estimate that only 30% to 39% of gun-owning American households with children store their guns locked and unloaded. A study published in 2000 estimates that in 1.4 million homes—households that include approximately 2.6 million children—guns are stored loaded and unlocked. Guns are most likely to be stored in this manner in households in the South, in households with teenagers, and in households where someone is employed in law enforcement.

The low safe storage rates in gun-owning households with children highlight the need for greater parent education and awareness about the risks that guns pose to children and youth. . . .

Misperceptions about children's ability to assess dangers and avoid guns may be one reason that many parents resist messages to store their guns safely or remove them from the home, even when children are clearly at risk. In one study published in 2000, gun-owning parents of depressed adolescents at risk of suicide were counseled by their doctors to remove firearms from the home. Only 27% did so. In a comparison group of parents who had depressed adolescents but who did not own guns when the study began, 17% acquired them over the next two years.

Nor have gun safety training programs been shown to increase safe storage practices. In fact, one study of gun owners found, "Individuals who have received firearm training are significantly more likely to keep a gun in the home both loaded and unlocked."

By and large, laws requiring adults to store guns safely also do not appear to be successful in reducing unintentional gun deaths among young people. Seventeen states have enacted these Child Access Prevention (CAP) laws, which make it a crime for adults to store guns negligently so that they are later accessed by children or adolescents. A 2000 analysis of 15 states with CAP laws found a 17% decrease in unintentional child gun deaths in those states, but the entire decrease was explained by one state, Florida, where the death rate fell by 51%. No other state with a CAP law experienced a statistically significant decline in unintentional firearm deaths among children. The study's authors theorized that Florida experienced unique declines because its law imposed the stiffest penalties of any state, its unintentional child gun death rate was unusually high prior to the law's enactment, and the law was highly publicized as Florida was the first state to enact a CAP law.

Parents Have to Be Proactive

Although CAP laws and programs designed to promote safe storage of guns have shown mixed results to date, parents still may be more promising targets for education and prevention efforts than are children and youth. . . . It is difficult to persuade children and adolescents to stay away from guns or behave responsibly around them. Young children and those in elementary school frequently lack the ability to judge their probable risk of injury, identify hazardous situations, spot ways to prevent injury, or apply safety lessons they have learned in a classroom to the real world. In one experiment, for example, preschool children and their parents attended a session in which a police officer discussed the dangers of guns and asked children to promise never to touch one. After the session, the children were videotaped playing in a room where toy and real guns were hidden. Despite their promises, the children who had attended the class found and played with real guns at virtually the same rate as children who had received no instruction.

Adolescents may have more of the cognitive maturity necessary to understand and apply gun safety lessons, but they also frequently have trouble assessing the risk of injury, and some are highly susceptible to peer pressure to engage in risky behaviors. Several researchers have documented that peer pressure plays a pivotal role in youth gun carrying; adolescents whose peers carry guns are more likely to feel the need to carry guns themselves. So far, the data evaluating programs that help adolescents to develop skills to resist peer pressure, make responsible choices about guns, and resolve conflicts peacefully do not show that the programs have been effective at reducing youth gun violence.

Thus, the potential of educational approaches aimed at children and adolescents appears to be limited, making it critical that parents understand the risks that guns pose to their children, and take action to shield their children from unsupervised exposure to guns. Policymakers, educators, and health care professionals should expand their efforts to promote stronger parental monitoring, as well as safe storage, so that children and youth do not have unsupervised access to guns.

Engaging Communities

Even the most vigilant parents cannot shield their children fully from exposure to gun violence among their peers, in their schools, and in their neighborhoods. Therefore, any strategy to reduce gun violence must engage communities in prevention efforts.

In some communities . . . social norms against violence have broken down, fostering conditions where youth gun violence can thrive. In these environments, many youth feel the need to arm themselves for self-protection.

To convince youth that carrying guns is not necessary or desirable, communities need to become safer. Because poverty, discrimination, and violence are often linked, one way to decrease violence is to address economic inequality and social injustice in the United States. Indeed, some believe this is the only way to reduce youth gun violence. . . .

Social Equality Is the Goal

Clearly, the economic and social factors that underlie youth gun violence must be addressed. Eliminating economic disadvantage and racism are important long-term societal goals, and would undoubtedly reduce youth violence while improving a broad range of outcomes for children. At the same time, however, policymakers and communities should not lose sight of a more proximate cause of youth gun violence; the guns themselves. One of the key factors in the rise of youth gun violence in the late 1980s and early 1990s was the diffusion of handguns into young people's hands. As researchers Jeffrey Fagan and Deanna Wilkinson have written, "The ready availability of guns in the inner city has undoubtedly shaped and skewed street codes toward the expectation of lethal violence."

Community leaders should take steps to change this expectation. They can promote young people's safety by sending unequivocal messages to youth that gun violence is not an acceptable way to resolve conflict. Elected officials, faith leaders, and educators all can play key roles in enforcing social norms against youth gun use. Because many youth who carry guns report obtaining them from family members and friends, community leaders also should send messages to adults that it is dangerous—to youth and to the broader community—to allow young people unsupervised access to guns.

A few communities have experimented with antiviolence initiatives that provide safe places for children to study and play, focus on community revitalization, and feature public awareness campaigns against gun violence. ... In Boston, for example, a coalition of African American ministers joined forces with police to send a forceful message—targeted at young gang members—that gun violence would not be tolerated in the community. Approaches like these have not been evaluated extensively, but they may hold promise for changing youth attitudes toward guns, empowering communities, and ultimately reducing youth gun violence.

Engaging youth themselves as agents for change in their neighborhoods also may be a promising strategy for reducing gun violence, and is being tried in some communities. For example, one program, Youth ALIVE! in Oakland, California, employs young people who were formerly involved in gun violence to work as mentors to youth who have been injured by guns. Programs such as these try to help youth create norms against gun carrying and gun violence in their communities.

Strengthening Law Enforcement

Stronger enforcement of existing laws against youth gun carrying is another strategy to reduce gun violence. Beginning in the early 1990s, some police departments adopted an aggressive approach toward identifying and punishing youthful gun offenders. Supporters of this approach argue that punitive law enforcement against the criminal use of guns is an effective way to deter gun violence. Indeed, at least one study found that fear of arrest can deter youth from carrying guns. Other observers maintain, however, that community-based policing strategies, which emphasize close collaboration between police and citizens to prevent crime before it occurs, may reduce youth gun violence more effectively over the long term. . . .

For example, New York City adopted an aggressive, punitive approach, and gun homicide rates declined. However, the drop came at the price of severe strains in relations with minority communities, which viewed the police tactics as racist. This made it more difficult for police to engage the community in youth gun violence prevention efforts.

In contrast, San Diego's policing strategy focused on stopping youth gun crime before it started by combining aggressive law enforcement with equally aggressive outreach strategies to engage the community in controlling crime and preventing youth gun violence. The San Diego police met frequently with community advisory boards to identify crime problems and discuss potential solutions. More than 1,000 citizen volunteers were trained to prevent crime and assist crime victims in their neighborhoods, and police officers were assigned to schools to assess at-risk youth and connect them with social services. Youth gun violence rates declined in San

Diego, and the city was spared the racial tension that plagued law enforcement efforts in New York.

It remains unclear how much police really can do to prevent or reduce youth gun violence, however. Analyses of gun violence rates in the nation's 20 largest cities suggest few differences from one place to another in the 1990s, regardless of whether police in those cities pursued punitive law enforcement strategies, community-based policing, a combination of approaches, or no specific policing innovation. Nonetheless, the San Diego example illustrates how police can partner with the community to communicate social norms against youth gun carrying and gun violence.

Organizations to Contact

The editors have compiled the following list of organizations concerned with the issues debated in this book. The descriptions are derived from materials provided by the organizations. All have publications or information available for interested readers. The list was compiled on the date of publication of the present volume; the information provided here may change. Be aware that many organizations take several weeks or longer to respond to inquiries, so allow as much time as possible.

American Civil Liberties Union (ACLU)
125 Broad St., 18th Fl., New York, NY   10004
(212) 944-0800 • fax: (212) 869-9065
Web site: www.aclu.org

The ACLU is an organization that works to defend the rights and principles delineated in the Declaration of Independence and the U.S. Constitution. It champions the collective interpretation of the Second Amendment; in other words, it believes that the Second Amendment does not guarantee the individual right to own and bear firearms. Consequently, the organization believes that gun control is constitutional and necessary in some instances. The ACLU publishes the semiannual *Civil Liberties* in addition to policy statements and reports.

Brady Center to Prevent Handgun Violence
1250 Eye St. NW, Suite 802, Washington, DC   20005
(202) 289-7319 • fax: (202) 408-1851
Web site: www.bradycenter.org

The Center to Prevent Handgun Violence was renamed the Brady Center to Prevent Handgun Violence in 2001. The organization also encompasses the Brady Campaign to Prevent Handgun Violence (formerly Handgun Control, Inc.), the Legal Action Center, and the Million Mom March. The Brady

Center aims to educate the public about gun violence, enact and enforce reasonable gun regulation, and reform the gun industry through litigation. The Brady Campaign works to enact and enforce sensible gun laws, regulations, and public policies through grassroots activism. It also works to elect public officials who support reasonable gun control legislation and to increase public awareness of gun violence. The Legal Action Center provides free legal representation for victims in lawsuits against gun manufacturers, dealers, and owners, and provides updates on recent gun lawsuits. The Million Mom March is a nonpartisan organization that fights to prevent gun violence.

Cato Institute
1000 Massachusetts Ave. NW, Washington, DC   20001
(202) 842-0200 • fax: (202) 842-3490
Web site: www.cato.org

The Cato Institute is a libertarian public-policy research foundation. It evaluates government policies and offers reform proposals and commentary on its Web site. Its publications include the Cato Policy Analysis series of reports, which have covered topics such as "Fighting Back: Crime, Self-Defense, and the Right to Carry a Handgun" and "Trust the People: The Case Against Gun Control." It also publishes the magazine *Regulation*, the *Cato Policy Report*, and numerous book-length studies.

Citizens Committee for the Right to Keep and Bear Arms (CCRKBA)
12500 NE Tenth Pl., Bellevue, WA   98005
(206) 454-4911 • fax: (206) 451-3959
e-mail: adminforweb@ccrkba.org
Web site: www.ccrkba.org

The CCRKBA is a gun rights organization that believes that the Second Amendment protects the right of individuals to buy guns. It disseminates gun rights information and lobbies legislators to prevent the passage of gun control laws. The

CCRKBA also sponsors the Citizen Action Project, which encourages individuals to get involved in the fight to preserve gun rights. The committee is affiliated with the Second Amendment Foundation and publishes several magazines, including *Gun Week, Women & Guns,* and *Gun News Digest.*

Coalition to Stop Gun Violence (CSGV)
1023 Fifteenth St. NW, Suite 301, Washington, DC   20005
(202) 408-0061
Web site: www.csgv.org

The CSGV and its sister organization, the Educational Fund to Stop Gun Violence, work to reduce gun violence and curb the power of the gun lobby through grassroots activism, a progressive gun control legislative agenda, and litigation against gun manufacturers. The coalition works with many other gun control organizations to lobby at the local, state, and federal level to ban the sale of handguns to individuals and to institute licensing and registration of all firearms. Its publications include various informational sheets on gun violence and the *Annual Citizens' Conference to Stop Gun Violence Briefing Book,* a compendium of gun control fact sheets, arguments, and resources.

Handgun-Free America
1600 Wilson Blvd., Suite 180, Arlington, VA   22209
(703) 465-0474 • fax: (703) 465-5603
e-mail: info@handgunfree.org

Founded in 2002, Handgun-Free America is a membership-based, nonprofit organization dedicated to the effort to ban private handgun ownership in the United States. It disseminates information on critical gun issues, such as the assault weapons ban, school and workplace shootings, and safe-storage laws.

Independence Institute
13952 Denver West Parkway, Suite 400, Denver, CO   80401
(303) 279-6536 • fax: (303) 279-4176

e-mail: anne@i2i.org
Web site: www.i2i.org

The Independence Institute is a public-policy think tank that supports gun ownership as both a civil liberty and a constitutional right. Through the institute's policy centers, it addresses subjects of importance through policy papers, opinion pieces, and special events.

The Johns Hopkins Center for Gun Policy and Research

School of Public Health, Baltimore, MD 21205
(410) 955-3995

Established in 1995 with funding from the Joyce Foundation of Chicago, the Johns Hopkins Center for Gun Policy and Research is dedicated to reducing gun violence. The center's faculty addresses gun violence as a major public health issue— focusing on prevention and recognizing the firearm as a vehicle of injury and death. By providing accurate information on firearm injuries, gun policy, and related research, the center serves as an important resource for policy makers, scholars, advocacy organizations, attorneys, the media, and the general public.

National Crime Prevention Council (NCPC)

1000 Connecticut Ave. NW, 13th Fl., Washington, DC 20036
(202) 466-6272 • fax: (202) 296-1356
e-mail: webmaster@ncpc.org
Web site: www.ncpc.org

A branch of the U.S. Department of Justice, the NCPC develops and implements programs that teach Americans how to reduce gun crime and to ultimately address the causes of gun violence. It provides readers with information on gun control and publishes educational materials on the subject of gun violence. NCPC's publications include the newsletter *Catalyst* and the book *Reducing Gun Violence: What Communities Can Do.*

National Rifle Association (NRA)
11250 Waples Mill Rd., Fairfax, VA   22030
(703) 267-1000 • fax: (703) 267-3989
Web site: www.nra.org

The NRA is America's largest organization of gun owners and the primary lobbying group for those who oppose gun control laws. The organization believes that gun control laws violate the U.S. Constitution and do nothing to reduce crime. In addition to its monthly magazines *America's 1st Freedom, American Rifleman, American Hunter, InSights*, and *Shooting Sports USA*, the NRA publishes numerous books, bibliographies, reports, and pamphlets on gun ownership, gun safety, and gun control.

Second Amendment Foundation (SAF)
12500 NE Tenth Pl., Bellevue, WA   98005
(425) 454-7012 • fax: (425) 451-3959
e-mail: adminforweb@saf.org
Web site: www.saf.org

SAF is dedicated to informing Americans about their Second Amendment right to keep and bear firearms. It believes that gun control laws violate this right. The foundation runs an attorney referral service for individuals in need of the services of a pro-gun rights attorney. It publishes the weekly newspaper *Gun Week*, the monthly newsletter *The Gottlieb-Tartaro Report*, the gun magazine *Women & Guns*, and the yearly *Journal on Firearms and Public Policy*.

U.S. Department of Justice
Office of Justice Programs, Washington, DC   20531
(202) 732-3277
Web site: www.ojp.usdoj.gov

The Department of Justice protects citizens by maintaining effective law enforcement, crime prevention, crime detection, and prosecution and rehabilitation of offenders. Through its Office of Justice Programs, the department operates the National Institute of Justice, the Office of Juvenile Justice and Delinquency Prevention, and the Bureau of Justice Statistics. Its publications include fact sheets, research packets, bibliographies, and the semiannual journal *Juvenile Justice*.

Violence Policy Center (VPC)
1730 Rhode Island Ave. NW, Suite 1014
Washington, DC   20036
(202) 822-8200 • fax: (202) 822-8202
e-mail: info@vpc.org
Web site: www.vpc.org

The VPC is an educational foundation that conducts research on gun violence and works to educate the public concerning the dangers of guns, and supports gun control measures. The center's recent publications include *United States of Assault Weapons; Really Big Guns, Even Bigger Lies*; and *Firearms Production in America*.

Bibliography

Books

Michael A.
Bellesiles

Arming America: The Origins of a National Gun Culture. New York: Knopf, 2000.

Shay Bilchik

Reducing Youth Gun Violence: An Overview of Programs and Initiatives Program Report. Collingdale, PA: Diane, 2004.

John M. Bruce
and Clyde Wilcox

The Changing Politics of Gun Control. Lanham, MD: Rowman & Littlefield, 1998.

Joan Burbick

Gun Show Nation: Gun Culture and American Democracy. New York: New Press: Distributed by W.W. Norton, 2006.

Philip J. Cook
and Jens Ludwig

Gun Violence: The Real Costs. New York: Oxford University Press, 2000.

Saul Cornell

A Well-Regulated Militia: The Founding Fathers and the Origins of Gun Control in America. New York: Oxford University Press, 2006.

Constance
Emerson Crooker

Gun Control and Gun Rights. Westport, CT: Greenwood, 2003.

Wendy Cukier
and Victor W.
Sidel

The Global Gun Epidemic: From Saturday Night Specials to AK-47s. Westport, CT: Praeger, 2006.

Alexander
Deconde

Gun Violence in America: The Struggle for Control. Boston: North-eastern University Press, 2003.

Susan Dudley
Gold

Gun Control. New York: Benchmark, 2004.

Derek Hinton

The Criminal Records Manual. Tempe, AZ: Facts on Demand, 2004.

David M.
Kennedy, Anthony
A. Braga, and
Anne M. Piehl

Reducing Gun Violence: The Boston Project's Operation Ceasefire. Collingdale, PA: Diane, 2004.

Gary Kleck

Point Blank: Guns and Violence in America. New York: De Gruyter, 2005.

Wayne LaPierre

Guns, Freedom, and Terrorism. Nashville: WND, 2003.

Wayne LaPierre
and James Jay
Baker

Shooting Straight: Telling the Truth About Guns in America. Washington, DC: Regnery, 2002.

Jeremy H.
Lipschultz and
Michael L. Hilt

Crime and Local Television News. Mahwah, NJ: Lawrence Erlbaum, 2002.

Barbara Long

Gun Control and the Right to Bear Arms. Berkeley Heights, NJ: Enslow, 2002.

John R. Lott Jr.

Bias Against Guns. Washington, DC: Regnery, 2003.

John R. Lott Jr.   *More Guns, Less Crime: Understanding Crime and Gun-Control Laws.* Chicago: University of Chicago Press, 1998.

Robert J. Spitzer   *The Politics of Gun Control.* 3rd ed. Washington, DC: CQ Press, 2004.

Peter Squires   *Gun Culture or Gun Control? Firearms, Violence, and Society.* New York: Routledge, 2000.

Josh Sugarmann   *Every Handgun Is Aimed at You: The Case for Banning Handguns.* New York: New Press, 2001.

George Tita et al.   *Reducing Gun Violence: Results from Intervention in East Los Angeles.* Santa Monica, CA: Rand, 2003.

Terrell Wright   *Home of the Body Bags.* Venice, CA: Senegal, 2005.

Maggie Wykes   *News, Crime and Culture.* Sterling, VA: Pluto, 2001.

Aaron Zelman and Richard W. Stevens   *Death by "Gun Control": The Human Cost of Victim Disarmament.* Hartford, WI; Mazel Freedom, 2001.

Periodicals

Michael Daly   "Yes, Virginia, Guns Kill Innocents," *New York Daily News*, April 17, 2007.

Vanessa Gezari   "Don't Blame Bullets on U.S., Shooting Victim Says," *St. Petersburg (FL) Times*, September 24, 2006.

Rachel Graves "Gun Debate Muzzles the Middle Ground," *Christian Science Monitor*, September 5, 2007.

D. Hemenway, D. Azrael, and M. Miller "Gun Use in the United States: Results from Two National Surveys," *Injury Prevention*, vol. 6, 2000.

Bob Hohler "Many Players Regard Firearm as a Necessity," *Boston Globe*, November 10, 2006.

Derrick Jackson "Democrats Still Silent on Gun Control," *Boston Globe*, April 25, 2007.

Dave Kopel "Guns and Politics, Together Again," *Los Angeles Times*, April 24, 2007.

Cathy Lanier and Vincent Schiraldi "Give Us Back Our Gun Law," *Washington Post*, March 15, 2007.

Christopher Lockwood "Is Gun Control Back? Did It Ever Go Away?" *Los Angeles Times*, April 23, 2007.

John Lott and John E. Whitley "Safe-Storage Gun Laws: Accidental Deaths, Suicides, and Crime," *Journal of Law and Economics*, October 2001.

San Francisco Chronicle "Politicians Duck the 'Gun Factor,'" October 4, 2006.

Alan Scholl "Who Is to Blame for the Virginia Tech Shootings?" John Birch Society, 2007. www.jbs.org/node/3495.

St. Petersburg (FL) Times "The Human Costs of a Gun Culture," October 4, 2006.

John Tabin — "A Disarmed Campus," *American Spectator*, Apr 17, 2007.

Washington Post — "Making Schools Safer," April 18, 2007.

Washington Post — "Time to Talk Guns," October 9, 2006.

Andrew M. Wayment — "The Second Amendment: A Guard for Our Future Security," *Idaho Law Review*, vol. 37, 2000.

Daniel Webster et al. — "Association between Youth-Focused Firearm Laws and Youth Suicides," *Journal of the American Medical Association*, August 4, 2004.

Daniel Webster and Marc Starnes — "Reexamining the Association Between Child Access Prevention Gun Laws and Unintentional Shooting Deaths of Children," *Pediatrics*, December 2000.

James Wilson — "Gun Control Isn't the Answer," *Los Angeles Times*, April 20, 2007.

Index